"James Ray has done a masterful job of taking complex truths and making them easy to understand and apply. The Science of Success *principles* have assisted a number of our top performers in accelerating and growing their business. Buy it, read it, and double your income."

Grant Sylvester
CEO, Money Concepts
Author, *The Money Gap*

"Success is the result of applying sound principles, which align with universal laws. This book is a powerful road map to guarantee your personal success."

Brian Tracy
Author, *The Psychology of Selling*

"James Ray is one of the most profound and impactful teachers I've ever worked with. He comes from a powerful place of practical technology and spiritual depth, a combination rarely seen."

Jack Canfield
Author, *Chicken Soup for the Soul* series

"James Ray has clearly defined the pathway to create a successful business and a successful life. Take action in any one of the numerous techniques discussed in The Science of Success and you will transform your life."

John Mike, M.D.
President, Global Holistic Medical Center
Author, *Brilliant Babies, Powerful Adults*

"This book will show you how to succeed in business and in life. It will help you achieve personal excellence and acquire professional significance."

Nido R. Qubein
Chairman, Great Harvest Bread Company

"James Ray provides us with all the tools necessary for the achievement of our goals. While he calls his study The Science of Success, *he has transformed his journey into a work of art, an understandable, workable, and powerful guide to interpersonal relationships."*

James C. Hansberger
Managing Director, Hansberger Group at Salomon Smith Barney
Author, *Nice Guys Finish Rich*

"Relationships and partnerships are key to anyone's long term success. The Science of Success *shows you how to leverage both in order to accelerate the achievement of your dreams."*

Tony Alessandra, PhD
Author, *Charisma* and *The Platinum Rule*

"James Ray is a master of many different disciplines. He not only knows how to make money and be prosperous in the business arena, but he is also an expert in many different spiritual disciplines. He's been there, he's done it, and he lives it."

Bill Harris
President and Director, *Centerpointe Research Institute*

"After reading The Science of Success, *you will not only have the how-to of success, you will understand why it works and will have the faith to go out and make it happen. James Ray has put together a masterpiece!"*

Richard and Sonja Palmer
President's Team Distributors, Herbalife International

"James Ray's content is superb! His knowledge and wisdom, and where he can take you with it, is incredible. The experiences he can give you is second to none."

Pete Bissonette
President and Publisher, Learning Strategies Corporation

THE SCIENCE OF SUCCESS

HOW TO ATTRACT PROSPERITY AND CREATE
HARMONIC WEALTH® THROUGH PROVEN PRINCIPLES

JAMES ARTHUR RAY

SUNARK PRESS
CARLSBAD, CALIFORNIA
WWW.JAMESRAY.COM

Publisher's Cataloging-in-Publication Data
Ray, James Arthur
  The science of success : how to attract prosperity and create harmonic wealth
  through proven principles / James Arthur Ray.

       p.   cm.

  Includes bibliographical references.
  ISBN: 0-9667400-0-9
  ISBN: 0-9667400-1-7 (pbk)
  1. Success. 2. Life skills. I. Title.
  BF637.S8 R39 2006   98-87858
  158.1 – dc21   CIP

Layout by Orange Pineapple Productions, LLC.

SunArk Press
Carlsbad, California
Printed in the U.S.A.

Third Edition

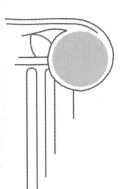

TABLE OF CONTENTS

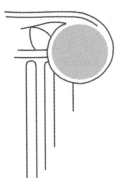

ACKNOWLEDGEMENTS

*"It is one of the most beautiful compensations
of this life that no man can sincerely try to
help another without helping himself."*
RALPH WALDO EMERSON

NOTHING OF VALUE IS EVER ACCOMPLISHED without the help of others. Through the efforts of the people that have been a gift to my life, this book becomes a reality to the world. There is a power that directs each of us to our unique life purpose, if we just take the time to listen to our higher-self. Thanks to all my friends, loved ones, and co-creators for listening to that unlimited power within. Most importantly, my heartfelt gratitude goes out to my Creator:

For giving curiosity and a passion for understanding to a skinny and insecure young boy who frequently wondered if his life would amount to much;

For bringing many great minds and mentors, formally and informally, into my life. Without them this book would not be possible;

For gifting me with parents who loved me, prayed for me, encouraged me, and believed in me even when I couldn't do so for myself. Mom and Dad, you are the greatest gift a son could ever hope for;

For sending Carol Costello, who saw the underlying message through outlines and rough scripts, and committed passionately to the project from day one. Your vision and voice have crafted my thoughts and ideas into the message the world is ready to hear. You are a joy to work with;

For bringing Dave Morton into my life, whose support, input

and creative ideas to further illustrate points has proven invaluable. Your belief and skills are treasured;

For allowing me to earn a wonderful livelihood, while living the life of my dreams and doing what I love;

And finally for you, the reader, and all my clients who aspire to continually grow and fulfill your God-given potential. Thank you for teaching me at least as much as I have taught you.

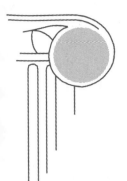

INTRODUCTION

"What lies behind us and what lies before us
are tiny matters, compared to what lies within us."
OLIVER WENDELL HOLMES

I WANT TO THANK YOU FOR CHOOSING TO explore the Science of Success. It has grown directly out of my personal experiences, my studies, and my seventeen years as a coach, professional speaker, and consultant to such companies as IBM, Coca-Cola, Merrill Lynch, Subway, Sprint, AT&T, Verizon, Century 21, Re/Max, Dow Chemical, Blue Cross/Blue Shield. It has literally transformed my life, and I believe it is the most effective and profound personal development program available today.

I have always been fascinated by why people like Gandhi, Einstein, and Martin Luther King succeeded in life, while other people who may have been equally talented and hard-working did not succeed. Why do some people always seem to win, to be "in the zone," while others do not?

My quest has been to find the principles that make people successful, so that we can all use them to become the people we are meant to be, to make our own unique contributions to the world, and to live the life of our dreams. I've spent two decades studying some of the most successful people in the world: people who were successful not only financially and in business, but in their personal, social, and spiritual lives. I read everything I could get my hands on, from ancient texts to contemporary philosophy, psychology, spirituality, and even quantum physics.

My gift is to be a synthesizer and a teacher. I have taken all this information and research, and looked at it in the light of successful people's lives and my own experience working with people. The Science of Success is the result. It lays out in a systematic, easy-to-follow way, the exact laws and principles that make people successful.

SUCCESS IS A SCIENCE

The principles in this program are nothing new. You have heard most of them before. What is unique about the Science of Success is that I have put this information together in a way that is understandable and usable by everybody! The Science of Success makes universal principles of success available and practical. Anyone on Earth can apply this science, and it will make them successful every time.

That's because the Science of Success works with universal laws, laws as fundamental and unbending as the law of gravity. If you follow these laws, I guarantee that you will succeed – every time, and in whatever endeavor you undertake – just as surely as a pencil will fall down instead of up when you drop it. People who win and succeed consistently use these laws and principles, whether or not they are aware of doing so. When you understand the Science of Success, you can choose to use them consciously. In doing so, you guarantee your success.

MY STORY

My interest in developing a Science of Success grew out of a life-changing event.

I didn't start out in a way that looked very successful. When I was growing up, I never dreamed that I would live in a beautiful house near San Diego, California, with views of the Pacific Ocean. I couldn't have imagined being one of the most successful sales managers at AT&T, or working with organizational expert Stephen Covey, or founding a business as successful and fun as mine!

In 1963, I was a small six-year-old boy in Tulsa, Oklahoma. I was excited because it was my first day of kindergarten. Like most kids, I loved anything new. I was a risk-taker. I wanted to go new places and do new things. I wanted to meet new people and find people who would love me. I had dreams. So I was thrilled to be starting kindergarten, but even on that first day, I began to realize something. I began to realize that I was different.

Remember the kid in your class who had big Coke bottle glasses and bucked teeth, the one everyone made fun of and pushed around? I was that kid. Young people can be cruel, even when they don't mean to be. They called me every name in the book, starting with "Four Eyes" and going all the way through "Bugs Bunny." As kids do, I took it very personally. I was hurt and began to withdraw inside myself. My self esteem took a beating, and I began to ask myself, "What's wrong with me? Why can't I be like everybody else?"

When I got to fifth grade, everybody started going out for sports. Athletes were very popular, and I saw my chance! I went out for every sport – baseball, football, and basketball – but I was skinny, gangly, and uncoordinated. I failed at every one, and that convinced me even more that I was not very cool and not very lovable.

I grew taller as I got older, but it soon became apparent that I wasn't going to fill out much. In high school, I was 6'1" and weighed 150 pounds. By then, girls had become very important, but I never had a date. Why? I never asked! Who would go out with me? I was the school nerd! In college, I continued the same pattern. No sports, no dates, no self esteem.

Then one Christmas, I got a free membership to a gym. I had always wanted to work out at a gym, but I'd never had the courage. I'd been afraid that people would make fun of me. But in my early twenties, I mustered up the courage to go to the gym, and I started working out.

An amazing change came over my body! I quickly went from being a 150-pound weakling to being a 230-pound, strapping, well-built young man. I got into the world of competitive body building, and my body kept changing. Just as importantly, my self esteem began to grow. I started to apply myself more, and I became more successful in my career. I attracted a new circle of friends, and I even had a date once in awhile.

But it was funny. I still felt an emptiness inside me, as if something was missing. I would be on a date and find myself thinking, "If she really knew who I was, she wouldn't give me the time of day." I'd think the same kind of thing about my new friends. "If they really knew me, they wouldn't have anything to do with me." Even though I looked great, had new friends, was dating, and was succeeding in my job, I was still running from the 150-pound nobody I thought I was inside.

I began to work out twice a day for two hours, to run even faster from that 150-pound weakling. All my energy was focused on building my body. Everything I ate, drank, did, believed, and thought was designed to make me a better bodybuilder. I did very well in the competitions, but it was never enough. There came a time when my body stopped responding to all the workouts, and I made a decision. I started injecting myself with dangerous doses of anabolic steroids. And I continued to grow.

THE WORLD TURNS UPSIDE DOWN

Then, in March of 1988, something happened that changed my life forever. On this particular day, I had just bought a brand new motorcycle. I remember thinking that it would bring me some more attention, and make me seem a little more cool. I jumped on the motorcycle that night and drove into downtown Kansas City, Missouri. Just as I was leaning into a hard right turn, I saw a set of headlights coming toward me.

I woke up in the Emergency Room in excruciating pain. Every bone in my left forearm was shattered, I had two herniated discs in my lower back, and both knees were blown out. Later they told me that the sound of the head-on collision had awakened people a block away. For the next six weeks, I lay in the Intensive Care Unit. I quickly went from a 230-pound strapping young man to a 170-pound, frightened, insecure human being.

The doctors told me that I would never be what I had been. I would never be able to bench press because my arm wouldn't support the weight. I couldn't work my legs because my knees were gone. I would never again have the physique that I thought made me who I was. That may sound ridiculous, but at that point in time, I honestly believed that my physique was who I was.

I went into the deepest depression you can imagine. I spent the next six months on disability, just lying on the couch and feeling sorry for myself. One morning I was lying on the couch watching TV, only not really watching, and a thought came into my mind. It was this: "Are you any different inside, with this body, than you were with the bodybuilder's body? Are your values and goals and dreams any different? Are you really a different person?"

At that moment, something changed. I saw that I was the same person that I'd always been, with the same character and the same values, goals, and dreams. I started waking up to who I really was, and promised myself I would never again deny that. I would never again put myself in the position to define myself by externals.

I began to read, to explore what we truly are as human beings. I began to get clearer about who I really was. I read hundreds of books on psychology, personal development, philosophy, quantum physics, and religion. I began to think in different ways, and my results began to change. I felt better about myself, and I did better in all areas of my life: in my career, my relationships, my inner life, everything. I went to seminars, listened to tapes, and took in huge amounts of new information. I got multiple promotions at work and became an upper-mid-level manager in a Fortune 500 company. I started earning a very handsome salary, and attracting new friends into my life who loved and supported me. They helped me grow.

When I was an upper-mid-level manager at AT&T, I left and started my own company. That was a stretch for me, and I was scared. But I did it anyway, and in the first year, my income tripled. I couldn't believe it!

What had happened? I had remembered who I was. That was the key to everything. I remembered that I was not my body. I realized that I was not my income or the things I had accumulated. I was so much more than those things, and I devoted my life to finding out more and more about who we all are. I wanted to know not just who we were, but how we could live and enjoy life to the fullest. How can each of us here on Earth make the most of our lives? How can we succeed in whatever we undertake so that we feel great about ourselves and about one another? How can we become the best that we can be and succeed in whatever we do?

THE ANSWER

After decades of research and working with thousands of people to maximize their potential, here is the bottom line: We live in an orderly universe that is governed by distinct and definite laws. Whenever we succeed, we succeed because we are living in alignment with those laws. When we do not succeed, it's because we are not living in alignment with those laws. It's just that simple.

The Science of Success lays out these laws in a systematic, easy-to-understand way. It gives you principles to help you apply those laws in your life. Everything about the Science of Success is designed to put the secret power of the laws into your hands, so that you can live the life you dream of living.

There may be times when you don't understand exactly how the Science of Success works, just as you may not understand exactly how electricity works. You don't have to understand how electricity works in order to flip the switch and turn on a light. I promise that if you study and apply the principles in this book, you will "flip the switch" and you will succeed.

Discovering who I am and how success happens has made all the difference in my life. It has made getting up each morning a joy. I have the relationships, the work, the house, and the life of my dreams because I live in harmony with universal laws.

My wish for you, and the purpose of this book, is that you have the same. God bless.

THE SCIENCE OF SUCCESS

"Success is the progressive realization
of a worthy ideal."
EARL NIGHTINGALE

YOU DESERVE TO BE PASSIONATELY ENGAGED in the life and work of your dreams, and to be successful in everything you do.

This book presents the universal Super Laws and Power Principles that make success inevitable, so that you can consciously choose to succeed in your profession, your relationships, your finances, your spirituality, and whatever else you undertake. When your personal passion collides with this scientific program for success, your dreams become real *every time*.

The subject of success has fascinated people for centuries, perhaps forever. But unfortunately, most people don't feel completely successful in their lives, and only a few actually achieve the success of which they are capable. Research and my own personal experience have shown me that when people consistently do not succeed, it's not because they aren't smart, or because they don't work hard, or because they aren't lucky. It's because they simply don't understand how success works. They don't understand the specific Super Laws and Power Principles that activate success.

WHAT THIS BOOK GIVES YOU

I have spent my entire adult life exploring why some people succeed while others do not. I've been captivated by Mahatma Gandhi's unbending commitment, by Martin Luther King's vision and passion, by Albert Einstein's sense of science and spirit, and by Napoleon Hill's willingness to give the secrets of building wealth to anyone who would read *Think and Grow Rich*.

I've studied these people and hundreds of others who were extraordinarily successful in personal, professional, financial, and spiritual arenas. I have studied the great literature and thinking on the subject, and seen how these people applied the Super Laws and Power Principles to succeed when other brilliant, committed, or passionate people did not. From these studies and my own experience, I have synthesized the formula that causes people to succeed.

No matter where you are today, this book is designed to take you to the next level of achievement and fulfillment. Success is your birthright. With the information in this book, it is yours for the taking. You will "crack the code" for success and learn to create exactly the future you want in a systematic and exciting way.

The Science of Success will help you discover the awesome power within you and show you how to unleash a potential for success that is greater than your wildest dreams. Not only can you achieve whatever level of success you want, I guarantee that you will do so if you understand and apply the universal Super Laws and Power Principles.

WHAT IS THE SCIENCE OF SUCCESS?

Some people think that success happens through luck, education, or hard work. Nothing could be further from the truth. Luck can help, and education and hard work certainly help – but these factors play a relatively small role in success. You probably know people who have worked very hard, or who are well educated or just plain lucky, but who are not very successful.

Success *never* comes by chance, education, or hard work alone. Success is a science. We live in an orderly system that operates according to distinct, specific, and predictable laws. Everything in our universe is organized and governed by these laws, from the smallest vibration of energy, to the ocean tides, to the entire cosmos, to your personal success. If you align yourself with these laws, you succeed *inevitably, every time.*

"Science," according to New Lexicon Webster's Dictionary, is "knowledge acquired by careful observation, by deduction of the laws which govern changes and conditions, and by testing these deductions by experiment."

That is exactly what I've done. I've observed successful people and what they do. I've deduced the seven Super Laws that govern their behavior and their success. I've tested those Super Laws and the Power Principles that unlock them in my own life. I've proven that they work for the thousands of people and organizations I've coached in personal and organizational development.

We will discuss each of the seven Super Laws in the next chapter. The seven Power Principles are the subjects of the next seven chapters. They are:

- The Power of Understanding
- The Power of Mindsets
- The Power of Vision
- The Power of Partnerships
- The Power of Giving
- The Power of Gratitude
- The Power of Accountability

These are not my principles or my laws. All I've done is put them together in a way that you can easily understand them, see how they relate to one another and to you, and use them in your daily life.

Whenever you have succeeded in any area of life, from childhood to the present moment, it's because you have lived and acted in accordance with these powerful laws. When you have not succeeded, you have not been living and acting in alignment with the laws. It's extraordinarily simple. If you want to make more money, have better relationships, be healthier, or meet your goals, you must understand these laws.

In addition to being universal, these laws are holistic. If you know how to use them in one area of your life, you can use them to succeed in *every* area. You won't be like the person who is financially successful, but not very healthy or happy. Or the person who has great relationships, but can't pay his rent. Or the person who makes a lot of money, but then loses it. Mastering the laws makes you successful in all areas and enables you to repeat your success time after time.

The universal laws operate all the time – whether or not you know about them, and whether or not they seem fair. It may not be fair that a youngster falls down when he is learning to walk, but the law of gravity is at work day and night, whether the youngster is sleeping or trying to take his first steps, and whether or not he even understands gravity. It's the same with the Super Laws. They operate in your life whether or not you know about them or use them consciously, so you might as well take hold of them and *put them to work for you*, steering your career, relationships, health, spirituality, and finances the way you want them to go.

The Science of Success combines these universal Super Laws with the seven Power Principles of action to create the Power of Seven. If you understand the Super Laws and use the Power Principles, you have all the resources you need to create the life you want. You have the power to choose your life and your future.

Many people believe that success is a specific result or outcome, a destination at which they arrive one day. They might define success as a certain amount of money in the bank, a certain kind of car or home, or a specific job, title, or relationship. These things may be part of your success – goals that you achieve along the way – but they are not success itself.

Success is more than the realization of one goal, or even several goals. Goals are vital to growth and life, and are an important way to measure your progress, but they are not "success." Getting that car, or that house, or that job doesn't mean that you have achieved success. These goals are stepping stones in your process – the means to an end – but not ends in themselves.

Success is not a specific destination; it is a *direction you choose*. It is a process, a never-ending journey. It is your constant progress toward your highest purpose, your vision, and the life of your dreams – in *all* areas. I know a lot of people who are highly success-ful in the financial arena but are not happy or fulfilled. They are not truly successful. Other people have great relationships, but are not succeeding financially. None of these people are truly successful.

Author and philosopher Earl Nightingale says that success is "the progressive realization of a worthy ideal." This means that it is an ever-unfolding awareness, an ever-growing wisdom.

Since success is a direction you choose, it is crucial that you know two things:

1. You need to know what you truly want from life, in your heart and soul.
2. You need to know that it is *your* direction, one that you your-self have chosen.

In my early twenties, I was working for AT&T. I was absolutely convinced that my job title defined my level of success. I became consumed by climbing the corporate ladder from position to position, and sacrificed a lot of personal and relationship time to achieve my goals. Eventually, I received a prestigious promotion and found myself transferred from my home town of Tulsa, Oklahoma, to Parsippany, New Jersey. I went from being a big fish in a little pond, to being a minnow in the ocean.

My "big promotion and title" left me standing in line at the copy machine to make my own copies, along with all the other people who had similar titles. My cost of living more than doubled, people weren't as friendly as they had been in Tulsa, and my social life changed dramatically. So the way that I and the people around me defined success didn't really work very well for me. It didn't make me happy.

You are the only person who can define success for you. Make sure you choose your *own* direction, rather than pursuing goals that society or other people tell you that you "should" want. If you don't, you may find yourself at the top of the ladder, but the ladder will be leaning against the wrong wall!

SUCCESS COMES FROM INSIDE, NOT FROM OUTSIDE

Success comes from within you. Some people argue that their level of success in life is determined by their circumstances, skills, environmental factors, or opportunities. Success may be *influenced* by these external or environmental factors, but it is not *determined or caused* by them.

It makes little difference what neighborhood you grew up in, how much money you currently have in your bank account, whether or not you like the job you have today, or whether or not you feel as if you are limited in any way. It doesn't matter how your parents did or did not treat you. It makes no difference if you are eighty years old or twelve, if you have a Ph.D. or never finished grammar school. It doesn't matter what work you are currently doing, if your relationships are on the rocks or absolutely phenomenal. History proves that literally hundreds of individuals with less that perfect circumstances have become highly successful in spite of what appear to be insurmountable odds.

Walt Disney is a great example. He was once fired from a job for not having enough creativity, and he was bankrupt six times before he went on to create Disneyland.

George Lucas was so broke when they finished making *Star Wars* that he couldn't even afford a poster for the movie premiere. Near the end of filming, when they were shooting the scene in which hundreds of people welcome the heroes home from the battle, they had almost no money to hire extras. They solved the problem by shooting the few people they could afford moving around one section of the huge hall. Then they stopped the camera, and had all those same people move down to another section of the hall, and shot them again. They repeated this process five times and then blended the sequences, so that with just a few people moving to different sections of the hall, they created the illusion of hundreds of extras and a hall full of people.

By the time shooting was over, George Lucas was very much in debt, but he never doubted his vision and his dream. He asked the studio if they would consider trading him the rights to toys and other *Star Wars* products so he could recover his debt, and they agreed. Over twenty years later, Lucas's companies have sold more than $1.5 billion in *Star Wars* toys.

With the profit from the toys, he built one of the finest special effects studios in the world, Industrial Light and Magic, and re-shot his *Star Wars* trilogy exactly the way he had originally intended. He re-released the films to rave reviews and introduced *Star Wars* to a new generation of fans. It was a number one movie, both in its first and in its re-release. Against all odds, Lucas believed in his vision and succeeded beyond his wildest dreams.

THE PAST DOES NOT EQUAL THE FUTURE

Many people get discouraged when they look at what has happened so far in their lives. They say, "I guess I just wasn't cut out to be a success. I've never really made anything work for me."

Every successful person knows that, when it comes to success, the past does not dictate the future. If you look at your current results to define who you are and how successful you can be, you may disempower yourself and even limit your future success. It's like driving to work and figuring out where to turn by looking into the rearview mirror instead of at the road ahead of you. It doesn't produce good results.

Your current situation is the direct result of your past thoughts, decisions, and actions. If you look at your current situation and make decisions about who you are and what you can have based on those results, then you are repeating the same thoughts, decisions, and perhaps even actions that got you where you are today. That does guarantee that you will get the same results again and end up with more of whatever you have now.

For instance, you may be making $25,000 and decide based on that, "Well, I'm the kind of person who makes $25,000." If you make that decision, you aren't likely to increase your salary much over the years. You may go up to $30,000 or even $40,000 over time, but you probably won't break into six figures until you let go of the decision that you are the kind of person who makes only $25,000 a year. Your past thoughts, decisions, and actions created that condition, but those thoughts, decisions, and actions have absolutely nothing to do with your future. If you continue to have the same thoughts and do the same things, then you'll get the same results. *But you don't have to think those thoughts or do those things again.*

When you change your thoughts, you will change your results. If you understand this principle, you can change your life. This is a new way of thinking for most of us. But true success begins only when you turn away from the things you *don't* want, and begin to focus on what you *do* want.

KNOW WHAT YOU WANT, NOT WHAT YOU DON'T WANT

Most people don't get what they want in life because they *don't know* what they want. They may have a vague idea, but they can't articulate clearly what true success means for them.

In fact, when I ask people what they want, nine times out of ten they tell me what they *don't* want. They say things like:

- "Well, I don't want to be broke anymore."
- "I don't want to miss my quota."
- "I don't want to work for the guy I'm working for now."
- "I don't want to argue with my wife."
- "I don't want any more credit card debt."

Those are good answers to the question, "What *don't* you want?" But I had asked them, "What *do* you want?"

There's a big difference between knowing what you don't want and knowing what you do want. That distinction is going to be the key to your success.

If you're thinking about what you *don't* want, that's what will show up in your life. What we think about, we bring about. So if you think consistently about what you *don't* want, then that's what will manifest in your world.

This is because the mind cannot process a negative. If you say to it, "Not peaches," it receives "peaches." If you say to it, "Not poor," it receives "poor."

Think about it. If I ask you not to think about a hot fudge sundae, what happens? Try it now. Don't think about a hot fudge sundae. Don't think about the ice cream or the gooey hot fudge sauce. Don't think about the whipped cream or the cherry on top. Do not think about a hot fudge sundae. What happened? If you are like most people, you had to hold the picture of a hot fudge sundae in your mind in order to try not to think about it. Probably the clearest image in your mind while you were reading this paragraph was a hot fudge sundae.

If I say to you, "Not red," what your mind latches onto is "red." If I say, "No scarcity," it latches onto "scarcity." You may be setting someone up for a fall if you tell them, "Don't spill the milk!" or "Don't slip on the ice!" What their mind receives is, "Spill the milk" and "Slip on the ice!" Whatever we focus on, we draw to us.

Besides, what you "don't want" may be highly inaccurate. I once worked with a client who told me that what he wanted was "not to be in debt." He told me that three times. Each time I asked him what he wanted, he told me what he didn't want. Finally, I said to him, "There are three guys who live on the beach near my home who are not in debt. They don't have cars, houses, apartments, or changes of clothes, and sometimes they don't even have enough food – but they don't have any debts. Is that what you want?"

"Well, no," he said. I worked with him for awhile, and he realized that what he really wanted was "financial freedom."

If you can change the habit of thinking about what you don't want and start thinking about what you do want, then I can tell you how to get it. If you can tell me "I want financial freedom," instead of "I don't want to be broke anymore" or "I don't want any debt," then I can show you how to move toward that goal.

Another thing that people do in response to the question, "What do you want?" is to tell me not what they want, but what they think they can get. This can also limit your results for two reasons. First, it may set your standard very low and put in motion a pattern of negative thinking. Second, it may not be what you really want, so there is no passion in the dream!

The human spirit will not invest itself in mediocrity, and you need that human spirit to achieve what you want. Your goal should be so exciting that you have butterflies in your stomach! That's how you unlock the power of the mind and put it to work for you!

DOING CERTAIN THINGS IN A CERTAIN WAY

If you think back to times in your life when you truly succeeded, whether in the business, financial, relationship, health, emotional, or spiritual arenas, you will see that you were doing things in a certain way.

If you are like most people, you may not even have known what you were doing that worked so well! Often, we aren't consciously aware of when we are "in the zone." It just happens. Before I understood The Science of Success, wonderful "wins" would often just drop into my lap. I had no idea where they came from or what caused them! *That meant I couldn't consciously make them happen again.* I just had to wait around to "get lucky."

I once heard a story about the great actor, Sir Laurence Olivier. He was playing Hamlet on Broadway, and one particular evening he gave such an extraordinary performance that the audience was mesmerized. When he delivered his last line and the curtain fell, they applauded so wildly that he came back for ten curtain calls. A friend of Olivier's was in the audience that night, and asked the stage manager to let Olivier know he was out front because he wanted to congratulate him. The stage manager went backstage to Olivier's dressing room and found him in a rage. The great actor kicked over a chair, spun, and knocked a shelf full of bottles onto the floor. Shocked, the stage manager asked, "What's the problem? You had the most incredible performance of your career!"

Olivier spun around. "I know I was fabulous," he yelled, still in a rage, "but I don't know *why!*"

That's where most of us find ourselves. Even when we succeed, we're not sure why. We don't know how we did it, so we're not sure we can repeat it. We have no idea what the formula was, so we have no idea if we'll ever succeed again. And sometimes we don't repeat it, or we lose the good that we have brought to ourselves, or we are successful in one area of life and not in another. We might manifest great financial success, for instance, but not create much abundance in the areas of health or relationships. Or we might have glowing good health and deep, wonderful relationships, but be unsatisfied with our income.

We can only become consistently successful when we understand what causes success and can repeat those patterns of thinking and acting *at will*. It's like having the combination to a lock: all the numbers and all the spins. If you do it right, the lock opens every single time!

This book will lay out that combination piece by piece, so that you understand each number and spin before going on to the next. When you work the formula accurately, there can be only one result. The lock opens. You succeed.

WISDOM IS BETTER THAN KNOWLEDGE

We're told that "knowledge is power" or "information is power." These statements aren't entirely true. Our world is full of knowledge. Between the internet and other exploding communication technologies, the information available to us doubles approximately every 2.5 years. Yet people don't feel very powerful in the world, or even in their own lives.

Not only that, but the people with the most knowledge and information are not always the most powerful or successful. Information is not power. It is nothing more than unorganized data. Knowledge is nothing more than organized information. Neither brings us true power or true success. To succeed today, we need more than information or knowledge. We need wisdom.

People who are truly successful are *wise*. Wisdom is the true power! I define wisdom as "information and knowledge that is organized, aligned, and acted upon in accordance with universal principles and laws." Whenever we act in a way that is organized, aligned, and in accordance with universal laws, we act wisely.

Wisdom is about *how* to think, rather than *what* to think. Truly wise people know how to gather pertinent knowledge about a subject and then listen to and apply the power of their intuition. They realize that the intuition, the "still, small voice" within, is our higher self asking to be manifest. Traditional education doesn't always teach us to use our intuition and emotions. We learn to read, remember, and repeat, but we don't always learn to think for ourselves. We are taught to operate more from memory than from imagination. Albert Einstein said, "Imagination is more important than knowledge."

When we combine information, knowledge, and experience with our intuition, we discover our own wisdom. a personal truth that synthesizes the head and the heart and puts us in touch with our higher self. In this wisdom, we understand that there is a reality greater than our physical world. Every culture and society has acknowledged some sort of unseen higher truth, higher purpose, and higher power. It has been called by many names, but the recognition of that higher presence is universal. Even quantum physics tells us that there is much more to life than meets the eye.

As a species, we human beings are becoming increasingly wise. As we begin to touch, understand, and work with this unseen realm, wisdom becomes more important than ever. It fact, it becomes the key to all success and greatness.

Even when people know what they want and act wisely, they don't always get what they want. This is usually because they don't feel that they deserve it. To make full use of the Science of Success, we must eliminate all thoughts of unworthiness.

We are all worthy of our highest good. When we forget this truth, we keep success at arm's length. Or we succeed once, but then won't let ourselves succeed again.

Many people look into their hearts and find glorious visions – to be a loving spouse, a successful entrepreneur, an inspiring leader, a great contributor to humanity – but they let these worthy ideals fall by the wayside because of limiting thoughts like, "I'm not smart enough," "I don't have what it takes," "Only bad people get rich," "I'm not good enough," or "I don't deserve it." They simply don't let themselves believe that they are worthy of all the good that they desire.

You are the only one who can transcend these kinds of limiting beliefs and come to a deep sense of worthiness within yourself. To "think worthy" and "act worthy," you must "feel worthy" and "be worthy." Here are some thoughts that may help you embrace that state of mind.

Most great religious, scientific, philosophical, and metaphysical works teach that we are God's creation. If we come from God, we must be part of God. If you don't like the word "God," substitute "energy," "universal mind," or "consciousness." It doesn't matter what you call it. If you and I come from God or energy or consciousness, then we must be part of that God, energy, or consciousness. And for that reason alone, we are worthy of the good we desire.

Think for a moment about the miracle that you are. With a single thought, you can control something as complex as raising your arm. All of the 157 muscles between your shoulder and your wrist work together in perfect harmony so that your desire is fulfilled.

Research has shown that each of us has enough energy in our body to light the entire North American continent for a week. If you were to convert that to kilowatt hours, you are worth literally billions of dollars.

Once you know that you are worthy of the good you desire, you can develop a personal vision that is worthy of you. I like to think of this personal vision as "your worthy ideal." It is your vision of what your life would look like if it were exactly the way you wanted it to be. In the course of this book, you will create that worthy ideal and fall in love with it. You will learn to fire it with high emotion and passion, so that it happens naturally and organically. Your worthy ideal becomes a foundation for all your efforts: something beautiful and magnificent that draws you forward and magnetizes you for success.

My personal vision is to deliver the Science of Success to every country on Earth, and to see people putting these concepts to work every day of their lives. This is a worthy vision and I am worthy of it. It is a cause that is bigger than I am and therefore pulls me continually forward. I am passionately in love with this cause and this vision. This is the kind of vision you will create: one that touches your heart, ignites your passion, and moves your very soul.

Your desires are God, energy, consciousness, or Supreme Intelligence wanting to express itself and its fullness through you. That's why Christ said, "It is your Father's pleasure to give you the kingdom."

I recently got an e-mail from Kate, who had been working with the Science of Success program for a few months. Her traditional upbringing had taught her that material, business, and financial success were somehow wrong, possibly even sinful. She learned the Super Laws and started applying the Power Principles. Most importantly, she came to see that, as she wrote me, "God truly wants me to have all the goodness that my heart desires and that life can afford." Her business doubled in less that six months, her financial results are the best in her region, she feels healthier physically, her communication with her family has improved, and she feels more connected with God and with herself.

God's greatest gift to you is your unlimited potential. Your greatest gift to God is to use that potential to the fullest. If you have a desire, you also have the ability to achieve that desire. Our highest intentions come from the God within, and that same God within never lacks the means to fulfill them.

A WORTHY PURPOSE

Feeling worthy and having a worthy purpose feed one another. Just as we must feel worthy to have a worthy purpose, we must have a worthy purpose in order to feel worthy. It's great to have a new house, a new car, or other material possessions, but do they really light up your heart? We deserve to be comfortable and have nice things around us, but what really feeds us is having a higher purpose in life: something larger than ourselves to which we can aspire and devote our energy.

The purpose of all life, from plants to people, is growth, advancement, expansion, and development. We have an inalienable right to the highest levels of development that we can achieve. We all have a burning desire to experience as much of our greatness and capabilities as we can. Sometimes that desire is stronger and more evident than at other times, but a yearning to be and do as much as possible lives within all of us. It's important to define and focus on these higher purposes for two reasons: it keeps our desire alive, and it makes us feel worthy of our good.

An insurance firm once hired me to design and create a new corporate culture. My associate Ken noticed that a claims clerk named Sally stopping working at 4:30 every day. She made her "to do" list for the next day, tidied up her desk, and finally clocked out at 5:00.

Ken approached her one day and asked, "Why did you quit working yesterday at 4:30 and not clock out until 5:00?"

"They won't let us leave until 5:00," she replied.

"What I meant was, why didn't you keep working until 5:00? There are still seven claims in your inbox."

She looked him right in the eye and answered, "They'll be there tomorrow."

After a moment of bewilderment, Ken asked, "What is the *purpose* of your company?"

She answered, "As far as I know, it's to make money." Ken then asked her if the company had a formal purpose statement.

"I think we have something hanging on the wall, but no one pays much attention to it," she said.

Finally he asked the obvious, "Does it motivate you?" She looked at him in disbelief.

"Are you kidding?" she asked.

Their current mission statement read: *Our mission is to maximize the return on investment for shareholders.* After working with the organization for eighteen months, one of the many changes was a new purpose statement that read: *the purpose of our enterprise is to reduce financial hardship and human suffering. To the degree we do that, we will prosper.*

Ken came back after eighteen months and saw the same clerk leave her desk at 4:35. At first, he was disappointed. Then he noticed that she went over and clocked out, returned to her desk, and finished five more claims before leaving. The next morning he asked her why she had worked overtime without pay.

"Our company is watching expenses," she replied. "I had five more claims to finish for the day."

"Wouldn't they have been there the next morning?" he asked.

"Oh, but they can't wait," she said. "There was a tornado in Oklahoma. Those poor people lost their homes. If I don't get them their money, they won't have a place to live."

A purpose is always more compelling than a goal. When you keep your higher purpose in mind, you will choose an ideal that is worthy of you.

FINANCIAL WORTHINESS

In my work, I come across many people who understand being worthy of abundance, except when it comes to one area: money. They don't usually say that they don't feel worthy in the area of finances. Instead, they say that they are satisfied with life just the way it is, or that they don't really want anything more than what they have.

My experience of working with thousands of people is that these sentiments are very temporary. They may not want anything more today, but they will want it tomorrow or the next day.

We are meant to have as much beauty, richness, pleasure, magnificence, and abundance as we can get from life, in every area! You would never say to your child, "You have enough education now. Stop reading!" You wouldn't say to a friend, "We have a great relationship, so I'd better ease off and stop working to make our love deeper." You wouldn't think, "I'm pretty healthy and fit, so I should stop exercising and start eating junk food." You wouldn't say, "My spiritual life is so strong that I'd better stop trying to improve my connection with my Source."

And you wouldn't justify these statements by saying, "After all, there are some people who are undereducated or who don't have good relationships or who don't have good health or strong spirituality. It just wouldn't be right for me to improve in these areas when I'm already ahead of others."

Yet this is exactly what some people do in the area of money. They find any excuse to hold their desires at arm's length.

To be truly successful, we need more than intelligent minds, loving relationships, and healthy bodies and spirits. We need financial well-being. Success is much more than money; it is experiencing the fullness of our true identity. But in our society, it is extremely difficult to experience all of who we are and to enjoy life fully unless we have the means to live comfortably. We need to be able to buy great books and have the time to read them. We must be able to travel and study other cultures, to listen to and understand great music, and to do whatever is important *for us* to do in order to become all that we can be.

George Bernard Shaw said, "It is a sin to be poor." The true meaning of sin is being out of harmony with who we are and the intuitive understanding that life is about expansion and growth. Shaw meant that, in today's world, it is difficult to grow into our completeness if we are poor.

THE BIG PICTURE

To succeed in life, we have to understand the big picture. The big picture is that our purpose as human beings is to create and express all that we can in life and to grow into our highest potential. Whenever we feel stuck or hampered in any way, we may be taking the small view of life or looking at just a tiny part of the whole panorama.

If we don't hold the big picture before us as we go through life, we don't draw from its energy and its power, and we may actually find ourselves engaged in activities that are counterproductive.

A manufacturing company that I worked with had an assembly line where people made telephones. At one end of the line, they made one small component for the phone that later became part of the complete instrument. They realized that they could save time producing their small piece of the phone by connecting one wire in a different way. They thought they were doing themselves and the company a big favor, but changing that one step fouled up work at the other end of the line. The result was lost time and a substandard telephone. They didn't understand the big picture. So in trying to expedite the process, they actually did a great deal of harm.

When we work within the big picture, we can't help but succeed.

AN INVITATION

I want you to get everything you can out of reading this book. To do that, you'll have to do more than just read. You'll need to take action. You'll need to take internal action to change how you *think* about success, and you'll need to take action in your life and in the world.

Action is the one thing that separates dreamers from achievers. If you take consistent, persistent, immediate, intelligent action to make these ideas work for you, I guarantee that it will supercharge your life in every way and that you will achieve your dreams. You'll see the world evolve and change right before your eyes, and you will know that you are the creative force behind that evolution.

Thinking about success doesn't really achieve much. You have to go out and do the footwork. To make a dream a reality, you must walk into your vision and *become* your dream.

I invite you to make that commitment now and to join me as we start exploring the seven Power Principles that help you put universal law to work for you.

SUMMARY
CHAPTER 1: THE SCIENCE OF SUCCESS

1. Success is a science governed by the specific, unchangeable laws of the universe.

2. You can put that science to work for you, if you are willing to:

   • Change your thoughts and attitudes

   • Realize that the past is not the future

   • Think and act wisely

   • Open yourself to your own worthiness

3. You don't need to understand all the details of the laws and principles. You just need to put them into action, much like flipping on a light switch without fully understanding the details of electricity.

4. In order to succeed, you must be clear on what you want in life – *not what you don't want* – and connect that worthy ideal to a higher purpose.

THE POWER OF
UNDERSTANDING

"Wisdom is the principal thing; Therefore get wisdom.
And in all your getting, get understanding."

PROVERBS 4:7

THE POWER OF UNDERSTANDING IS THE FIRST OF SEVEN Power
Principles that enable you to create the life of your dreams through
The Science of Success. The Power of Understanding includes all of
the information you have just read in Chapter 1, plus the seven
Super Laws that we will discuss in this chapter.

These Super Laws are like gravity. They are at work in every cen-
timeter of the universe, all the time, whether or not you are aware
of them. When you understand them, you can put them to work
for you deliberately in your personal life, your work, your finances,
your relationships, your spiritual pursuits, and every other area.

The seven Super Laws, together with the seven Power Principles
that help you harness their energy, form the Power of Seven. When
you align your life with the Power of Seven, success is inevitable.

THE SEVEN SUPER LAWS

We learned in Chapter 1 that our universe is an orderly place. It is
governed by exact and consistent laws. To the extent that we align
ourselves with these laws and apply them using the seven Power
Principles, success is guaranteed.

Actually, the seven Super Laws are applications and expressions
of the one great law revealed to us by quantum physics: *Everything
is energy.* This means that the things we believe to be solid – a car, a

couch, this book – are actually, at the quantum level, simply impulses of energy and information.

The seven Super Laws are subsets of this one great law. They govern our lives and everything in the universe. I call them the Super Laws because they work everywhere, for everyone, all of the time. They are so precise that they allow us to send people to the moon and time their landing back on Earth to within a fraction of a second.

You don't need to memorize the Super Laws, and you don't need to understand them at the same level of detail that a nuclear physicist might. You just need to understand the basic principles and get a sense of how they work in your life, much like you don't need to understand everything about the law of gravity in order to use the information that things fall down, not up.

These seven Super Laws, and the seven Power Principles that help you apply them, will catapult your personal and professional life to levels of joy, fulfillment, and success beyond your wildest dreams. If you want to succeed month after month, year after year, you must understand these Super Laws and Power Principles. Let's look at the Super Laws one at a time.

SUPER LAW #1: THE LAW OF PERPETUAL TRANSMUTATION OF ENERGY

This Super Law tells us that energy is always moving, transmuting, and changing. It takes one form, then another, but it never stands still. Everything we see, hear, taste, touch, or smell is in a constant state of change. In fact, this Super Law tells us that *change is all there is*.

Everything is energy, and energy is motion. So even things that appear completely solid and stable – an antique table, a concrete skyscraper, a chunk of lead – are constantly changing. If you put samples of these substances under a microscope, you can actually *see* that they are changing into a different form right before your eyes.

People sometimes say, "Let's wait until the dust settles after all this change before we do anything," or "I just want this change to hurry up and be over so I can get back to normal!" They don't understand that *change itself* is what's normal!

Cultural clichés often represent a truth that has been passed from generation to generation. "You can't go home again," is a statement of The Law of Perpetual Transmutation. You really can't go back, because your home changed the minute you left, and so did you! Every cell in your body is replaced in less than a year. You aren't even the same physical person you were a year ago. You can go back to your old house or your old town, but it won't be the same, you won't be the same, and your relationship with it won't be the same as it was. In fact, the whole world as we know it is gone the moment we know it!

Futurist Eric Hoffer says, "In times of change, the learners will inherit the earth, while the learned find themselves beautifully equipped to deal with a world that no longer exists."

SUPER LAW #2: THE LAW OF VIBRATION

This law states that everything in the universe – from a thought to a mountain, from the smallest electron to the entire cosmos – is in a constant state of vibration. The levels of vibration vary, and we call the most intense vibrations the higher frequencies. Rocks, people, the Earth, and the universe are all energy, vibrating at different frequencies.

Thought is one of the most potent forms of energy, vibrating at one of the highest frequencies. Just as x-rays and gamma rays can penetrate "solids," thought waves can penetrate not only "solids," but also time and space. This means that *your thoughts are actually things*. Every thought creates a vibration, an impulse of energy that goes out into the cosmos and stays there forever. When you think something, that thought is just as real as the book you are holding in your hand.

Have you ever noticed the feeling in a room when people are

under stress? Have you ever felt the vibration change when someone walked into a room? Have you ever passed by someone you didn't even know and felt a strange energy? A friend and I walked into our post office recently carrying armloads of mail. We passed a woman coming out and felt washed over by a wave of anger. We looked at one another and asked, "Did you feel that?" Our friendly postman confirmed our experience when he told us about the verbal abuse he had just received from that woman.

The Law of Attraction is a subset of the Law of Vibration. It states that things which vibrate at similar frequencies attract one another, and things that do not vibrate at the same frequency repel one another. Two drops of water attract one another and merge into one. A drop of oil and a drop of water repel one another because they are of different vibrations. The Law of Attraction is how we most often see the Law of Vibration manifesting in our physical world. It is why we attract to us the things we focus on, think about, and give energy to.

Bottom line, the Law of Vibration and the Law of Attraction tell us this: *What you think about, you bring about.* According to the Law of Attraction, you are not who you think you are. You *think* who you *are.*

When you think positive thoughts, you attract positive people and circumstances to you. When you think negative thoughts, you attract negative people and circumstances. Like attracts like. Every thought you think attracts to you things that are like itself. Your thoughts can attract your dreams or your fears. If you think about your dreams, you will attract them. If you think about your fears, you will attract the things you fear. The choice is entirely yours.

You naturally move toward what you focus on and move away from anything that is unlike the thoughts you are thinking. If you spend 90% of your time focusing on what you *don't* want, you will move toward that. If you think about what you do want, you will move toward that. By the same token, you can repel negativity by thinking positively. Have you ever felt so good that nothing negative could get to you? That's the Law of Attraction as well.

Warren Bennis talks about this phenomenon in *Leaders: Strategies for Taking Charge*. He calls it the "Wallenda Principle." A few months before high-wire artist Karl Wallenda fell to his death, he had a nightmare about falling off the high wire. Prior to the nightmare, he had never felt fear. He had devoted all his energy to creating new, more thrilling stunts. But the nightmare focused his attention on not falling. His widow said that, after that dream, he became obsessed with not falling. He checked the equipment constantly and lived in fear of tragedy. A few months later, he fell to his death.

Whatever you feed with your attention grows. Some people even see this with their houseplants. They play music and talk to them, and the plants flourish. It's not necessarily the music or the words that are spoken, but the energetic attention that makes the plants prosper.

Napoleon Hill, the great student of success and human potential, said, "Any idea that is held in the mind that is emphasized, feared, or revered will begin at once to clothe itself in the most convenient and appropriate physical form that is available."

Much of the Science of Success is based on the Law of Attraction, and we will use this term interchangeably with the Law of Vibration in our discussions.

SUPER LAW #3: THE LAW OF RELATIVITY

First of all, you do not need to understand the whole of Einstein's Theory of Relativity to use the Science of Success! You just need to understand its metaphysical implications, which are actually very simple.

This law tells us that everything in our material world is only made real by its relationship to something else. "Hot" only exists because we compare it to "cold." I went skiing recently and my hands got very,

very cold. When I came inside and ran cold water over them, it actually felt warm in comparison to how cold my hands were! In the same way, "good" only exists in comparison to "bad."

In fact, everything in life "just is," unless and until we compare it to something else. Nothing in life has any intrinsic meaning, except the meaning we give it. Another way to state this Super Law is: *Relationships are everything, and everything is due to relationships.*

We can use this Super Law to see how some of our comparisons may be self-defeating. Beth is an attorney at a large law firm, and she complained constantly about how little money she made and how terrible her financial condition was. I said to her, "Do you realize how wealthy you are compared to people in Bangladesh, where the annual income is approximately $180?" This made her stop and think. She began to think of herself as being quite prosperous, and those thoughts attracted more prosperity to her.

How you choose to compare yourself and your success either pulls you up or holds you down. If you choose to pull yourself up by letting the Law of Relativity help you find the good in life, then you must succeed.

SUPER LAW #4: THE LAW OF POLARITY

The Law of Polarity states that nothing can exist without its opposite. If hate exists in someone, then love must exist as well. If you see low potential in someone, then high potential must also exist in that person. "Failure" in life must be accompanied by the seeds of success. If something is really awful, then the possibility must exist for it to be awesome!

Further, the Law of Polarity states that, in fact, these opposites are simply different manifestations of the same thing!

Napoleon Hill said, "Every failure carries the seed of an equivalent or greater benefit." My "failures" have been some of the most powerful experiences of my life, and they have given me the tools

I needed to succeed. Without failure, it is difficult to know success. Babe Ruth held the world record for home runs, while at the same time holding the world record for strike-outs.

When you hear successful people talk about how they got where they are, what do you hear? Do they say that they just opened their eyes one morning and success was all around them? No. Their stories are full of how their failures taught them and directed them toward success.

You may have heard the story about the young man who asked the wise man, "How did you get to be so wise?"

"By making wise choices," the wise man answered.

"How did you know they were wise choices?" the young man countered.

"Why, by experience, of course," the old man replied.

"How did you get experience?" the young man asked.

"By making poor choices!" the wise old man exclaimed.

Knowing that every challenging experience contains the seeds of its opposite, success, makes life a constant learning experience and a great adventure.

SUPER LAW #5: THE LAW OF RHYTHM

The Law of Rhythm states that the energy in the universe is like a pendulum. Whenever something swings to the right, it must then swing to the left. Everything in existence is involved in a dance: swaying, flowing, swinging back and forth. Everything is either growing or dying.

High tide sweeps in, and low tide sweeps out. The moon rises, and the moon sets. The seasons come and go. Even our moods and levels of awareness swing back and forth. We have highs and lows: intellectually; emotionally, and physically. Everything from relationships to the stock market goes through cycles, yet everything has a rhythm, a pattern. What may sometimes appear to be random is actually very orderly.

Great leaders have used their understanding of this Super Law to predict their own declines or their greatest victories. When something is at its peak, they realize that it will soon start to swing back the other way. You probably use this Super Law without even being aware of doing so. If you've been putting out a lot of effort toward marketing in your business, you may sense at some point that you need to stay closer to the office and make sure your organization is delivering on its promises. If you've been doing a lot of training and working out, your body may need a rest. This Super Law shows up in everyone's lives, even in the act of going to sleep and waking up. You use it when you get a gut feeling or an intuitive response to whether this is a good time to act or whether you should sit tight and wait.

The more deeply you understand this Super Law, the more astute you become in assessing situations and knowing what to do.

SUPER LAW #6: THE LAW OF CAUSE AND EFFECT

Most of us are already familiar with this Super Law. It states that every effect must have a cause, and every cause must have an effect. Anything that is a "cause" is actually the "effect" of something that came before it. And that "effect" becomes the "cause" of something else. It is impossible to start a "new" chain of events. This Super Law shows us the universe is a perpetual and never-ending cycle.

All the great religions and philosophies speak of the Law of Cause and Effect. They phrase it in a variety of ways:

- What you sow, so shall you reap.
- If you put a lot out, you get a lot back.
- You can't get back something other than what you give.
- You can't grow potatoes by planting corn, and you can't reap diamonds by planting rocks.

- What goes around, comes around.

- As you give, so shall you receive.

The fundamental idea in the Science of Success is this: What you think about, you bring about. This is the ultimate in cause and effect, and it can happen not just in your own life, but in organizations.

In 1991, I was hired by a manufacturing organization to improve employee morale, which had hit an all-time low. It turns out there was a reason for all the bad feelings. I discovered shortly after I arrived that the plant was scheduled to close and everyone had just been told they would be out of a job. No wonder people were unhappy! I knew that to improve morale, I had to get them to change their thinking.

It was a hard sell, but I told them repeatedly and passionately, "If you continue to focus on what you don't want, going out of business, you'll just speed along the process." Every day, in a variety of ways, I encouraged each individual to focus on what he or she wanted to create. I asked them constantly, "What do you want?" When they answered with something they didn't want, I said, "I know that's what you don't want, but what do you really want?"

Finally, I began to get through. They started to set goals and to get excited about them. Rather than focusing on "not going out of business," they began to focus on "becoming profitable and acquiring new customers." Rather than focusing on "how wrongly we were treated," they began to ask, "How can we make today a fun and productive day?"

By concentrating on how awful it was that the plant was shutting down, they had actually been helping to attract that reality. When they decided that if they were going out, they might as well go out with style, three things happened:

1. They started to feel good about themselves and their accomplishments.
2. They became very attractive and productive employees who were high on the list of people to transfer to other parts of the company that were not closing.
3. The entire plant became more productive.

Slowly, we began to see changes. The primary production line met its quota for the first time in months. People began to take pride in their work again. A new slogan started circulating around the plant: "We're gonna make it happen... no matter what!" We celebrated the small successes and talked about how to be even better.

One day, management made a huge announcement that changed everything. The plant had recruited a new client and had a two-year contract. They were going to stay open! It took awhile to shift the mentality of an entire organization, but six years later they still have their doors open and are a profitable business. What they thought about, they brought about.

Nothing in your life happens by accident. When you succeed, there is a specific cause for your success. You can identify this cause by looking to see which Super Law is operative and then applying it again to produce success once more.

SUPER LAW #7: THE LAW OF GENDER

This Super Law governs what we call creation. It states that male and female, yin and yang, must unite in order for creation to take place. Further, this law says that everything must have an incubation or gestation period. A baby takes nine months. Plants, trees, flowers, and corn all have their respective gestation periods.

The implication is that everything "new" is merely the result of things that already existed changing form. In this sense, nothing is ever created or destroyed. It just changes form to recreate itself, in the same way that a baby is generated by sperm and egg coming together. The "new" baby is the result of cells from the mother and father changing form and recreating themselves.

The way this Super Law relates to your success is that *all the success you want in life already exists*. There is only one source of supply. Everything comes from and is made up of the same energy. Therefore, the good that you desire already exists. It may currently be in a different from, but it is here nevertheless. There is nothing to create. All you need to do is access it and manifest it. This book will show you exactly how to do that.

This Super Law calls on us to remember that we are spiritual beings, and that the physical world we experience is only a small part of our true existence. To become successful and stay successful, we must stay connected with the source of all success. We must have faith in this unseen reality. True faith is the ability to believe in and trust in the unseen. Rather than waiting until you see it to believe it, begin to believe it until you see it!

We do this more easily and often than we realize. At this moment, the room you are in is full of radio waves. You know those radio waves are there, even though you can't see them. You know that if you turned on a radio and tuned it to a particular station, you could hear them. *You just have to tune in to the right frequency.* To get the music you want in your life, your highest success, you just have to tune into the right station and lock on!

But remember, everything has its gestation period, and we don't always know how long that gestation period is on the unseen, non-physical plane. On the physical plane, we know that it takes nine months to have a baby. It would be ridiculous for the father to go up to the mother in her third month and say, "Where's the baby!? Is this going to work or not?" Yet that's just what we often do when we're working on the non-physical plane, because our information isn't quite as exact in that realm as it is in the physical world.

I've found that people who do not win in life, nine times out of ten, give up just when something is about to break open for them. They've planted the seed, they're waiting for it to manifest, it's just about to break through the ground, but then they lose patience and say, "It's not coming!" They give up and throw away the chance to have what they really want.

Belief and faith play a vital role in the Science of Success. The great teacher, Deepak Chopra, speaks about the agony he went through when he was trying to create his medical school. He asked his mentor where the money was going to come from, and his mentor replied, "From wherever it is at the time." His mentor knew that Chopra's success already existed, albeit in a different form. That kind of faith brings forth miracles.

Plant the seed, and then have faith and wait. Your success will come, just as surely as the baby does after nine months. You just have to turn on your radio and tune in to the right frequency. What you are seeking is also seeking you.

THE SEVEN POWER PRINCIPLES

The Power of Understanding encompasses all the material you have read so far. It includes both the general principles we discussed in Chapter 1 and the seven Super Laws we covered in this chapter.

It is the first of seven Power Principles that will help you align with the Super Laws. The other six Power Principles will be covered in the following chapters. These Power Principles are designed to be used by people just like you. They are the action steps you take to open the combination lock that holds the life of your dreams. The Super Laws are the numbers in that combination, and the Power Principles are the spins. When you have both the numbers and the spins, the combination lock will open for you every time.

1. The seven Super Laws are all subsets of the one primary law of quantum physics: Everything is energy.

2. The Super Laws are:

   - *The Law of Perpetual Transmutation of Energy*: Energy is constantly changing and transmuting, and change is all there is.

   - *The Law of Vibration:* Everything in the universe, seen and unseen, vibrates at various frequencies. Thought is one of the higher frequencies, or the most potent form of energy. The subsidiary Law of Attraction tells us that like attracts like, and that we draw to us the things on which we focus and to which we feed energy.

   - *The Law of Relativity*: Everything that exists is defined by its relation to something else. Everything "just is" until it is compared.

   - *The Law of Polarity*: If one thing exists, its opposite must also exist. Failure must be accompanied by the seeds of success.

   - *The Law of Rhythm*: There is an order, flow, or pattern to all movement. Life is a dance.

   - *The Law of Cause and Effect*: Everything has a cause and a corresponding effect, and every effect has a corresponding cause.

   - *The Law of Gender*: There is nothing new in the cosmos. All things manifest according to their individual gestation period.

THE POWER OF MINDSETS

"To ignore the power of paradigms to influence your judgment is to put yourself at risk when exploring the future. To be able to shape your future, you have to be ready and able to change your paradigm."

JOEL ARTHUR BARKER

WE HAVE SEEN THAT THOUGHTS ARE THINGS, and that we draw to us physical realities that reflect our thoughts. If we think negative thoughts, we attract negative people and circumstances. If we think positive thoughts, we become magnets for positive people and situations. Our success literally depends on the quality, frequency, and intensity of our thoughts.

If we aren't succeeding in any area, we need to take stock of our thoughts. We may be operating with outdated and limiting ideas, habits, practices, attitudes, values, beliefs, and expectations. These old mental patterns keep us stuck in lack and limitation, so we must replace that old negative programming with thoughts that allow us to be, do, and have all that is available to us in life.

Power Principle #2, the Power of Mindsets, shows you how to release those old mental patterns and build new ones that take you where you want to go in life.

WHAT IS YOUR MINDSET?

Our mindset (or sometimes called our paradigm) is the sum total of our beliefs, values, identity, expectations, attitudes, habits, decisions, opinions, and thought patterns – about ourselves, others, and how life works. It is the filter through which we interpret what we see and experience. Your mindset shapes your life and draws to you results that are an exact reflection of it. What you believe will happen, happens.

We approach, react to, and literally create our world based on our own individual mindset. Our mindset tells us how the game of life should be played, and it governs whether or not we play it successfully. We might have a mindset, for instance, that tells us, "Life is very hard, and I have to struggle just to stay even." Or we might have a more positive mindset, like, "I'm great at what I do and people want to work with me."

Thoughts are powerful magnets. Whatever our mindset tells us is what we attract, whether or not we're even aware of what our mindset is! If you have the belief that, "Life is very hard and I have to struggle just to stay even," for example, you don't have to be aware of that belief in order to experience struggle. If fact, if you want to see what your mindset really is, you have only to look at your life and your results. The Bible tells us, "According to your beliefs it shall be done unto you."

When we don't examine our mindsets and question whether they support us or limit us, we are operating "on automatic." We are no longer choosing our beliefs and mindsets, but they neverthe-less cause us to live a certain way. *We create our own mindset, but at some point, our mindset creates us.* If we don't question a belief that "life is hard," for instance, we are going to keep struggling without even knowing why.

We all have old beliefs lurking around. Many of them were picked up in childhood and no longer serve us or contribute to our success. When Alice started examining her mindset, she realized that she had a belief that "Money comes from my parents." When she was a child and wanted ice cream, toys, or dolls, that's where the money had come from. As a teen, that's where her allowance had come from. As an adult, she often found herself in financial trouble and had to borrow large sums of money from her parents.

Joel Arthur Barker writes in *Paradigms*, "To ignore the power of paradigms to influence your judgment is to put yourself at risk when exploring the future. To be able to shape your future, you have to be ready and able to change your paradigm."

Our mindsets drive our behavior. If you want to get a good look at your own mindset and those of your family and friends, try having a friendly family card game during the holidays. The chances are, people will do around the card table whatever they do in life. Do some people act bored? Competitive? Easy going? Do they want to save face or be cool, or will they risk alienating people in order to control and dominate? Are they shy or overbearing? How do they believe others will act toward them? Do some people think they'll be taken advantage of or made to look silly? Do they think others are stupid or behaving badly? All of these behaviors reflect certain mindsets, ways of looking at oneself, others, and the world.

We can believe whatever we want to believe. And we can find a lot of evidence to support whatever belief or mindset we choose, so we might as well choose beliefs that empower us and move us forward. We start succeeding when we understand that we have a choice because, at that point, we can start selecting beliefs that take us where we want to go. William James, the father of modern psychology, said, "Believe that your life is worth living, and your belief will create the fact."

To be successful, you have to understand your mindset. You have to bring it to the conscious level, take a good look at it, and see if there is anything you want to change. Otherwise, your hidden beliefs will drive you. If you don't know what they are, you can't do anything about them.

If you want to change your results, you must change your mindset.

A mindset shift means changing from one mindset to another. In the Science of Success, it means shifting from a mindset that impedes our success to a way of thinking that encourages and magnetizes success.

When you shift your mindset, you change to a new game and a new set of rules. When your game and rules change, your whole world starts changing. You begin to put out a different energy, so you attract new kinds of people and situations into your life. When you transform your thinking, you transform your world. Oliver Wendell Holmes once said, "Man's mind stretched to a new idea never returns to its original dimensions."

Many people say they want to change their lives. They go hear a motivational speaker or make a New Year's resolution and get very excited about all the changes they see for themselves. Or they go to a seminar or read a book and see that they want to start doing things differently. They may even make a few changes in the first couple of weeks. But then their energy seems to lag. Their enthusiasm plummets. Before you know it, they are back in their old rut. When this happens, it's because they were trying to manipulate the effects in their lives, rather than addressing the cause. *They were trying to change their results without changing their mindset.*

To produce dramatic and permanent results, you have to change the way you think. Unless there is a mindset shift, any change or improvement will be minimal and/or short-term.

A SIMPLE SHIFT

Rich worked in the financial securities industry, and he hired me as his personal success coach. He was very excited about the sales techniques and business strategies I suggested, and we came up with some great ideas to move him toward his goals. The odd thing was that Rich never implemented any of these plans.

I knew the problem must be in his mindset, and we began to explore his underlying beliefs about himself and the world. Rich had grown up in a family that emphasized a stable job and security. It didn't matter how much money you made, you were supposed to, "live within your means and don't risk leaving a secure job for an opportunity that might fail." He had also grown up hearing that it was, "easier for a camel to pass through the eye of a needle than for a rich man to enter the kingdom of heaven."

These two beliefs were clearly holding him back. To grow his business in the ways that he wanted it to grow, Rich was going to have to take risks. And somehow, he was going to have to believe that his success would benefit everyone around him and not keep him out of heaven.

Rich and I looked for ways that he could change his mindset and found ourselves talking about how much he enjoyed such adventurous activities as hiking, skiing, and rock climbing. He saw that taking risks in business was just another way for him to experience this kind of adventure and excitement. By changing his risk mindset to one of adventure, Rich found it much easier and more fun to take those risks necessary to grow his business.

Rich also experienced some things that helped him start changing his beliefs about wealthy people. He had a fiancée whom he wanted to shower with gifts and employees he cared about who would do well if he succeeded. He wanted to send his parents on a cruise they'd always wanted to take. He began to see that it was not the money itself that was good or evil, but what people *did* with the money, and he began to welcome the prosperity that his business could bring him. Three months after choosing his new mindset, Rich's business generated quarterly revenues that were more than the preceding year's annual revenues!

Changing his mindset changed his life. It's great to seek out new approaches, skills, and techniques in business and in your personal life, but they only work when they are laid on a foundation of new thought.

If you want to change the effect, you have to change the cause, and our thoughts are the ultimate cause. If we try to change limited income, limited satisfaction, or limited relationships by concentrating on *them* instead of changing the thoughts that caused them, we don't get very far. We need to go back into the unseen, unlimited world of thoughts and feelings and make our changes there. Then our new thoughts, rather than our old thoughts, will project into the physical world.

In other words, take your attention off any lack or limitation in your life right now: your bank account, your house, your job, your relationships, or whatever. These things are only the residuals of your past thinking. When you focus on what you already have, you will only create more of the same.

Instead, start putting your attention on what you *do* want in your life. Work with cause, rather than trying to manipulate effect. My client John began creating miracles when he understood this concept. His six employees had all developed the habit of coming in late. Instead of arriving at 9:00, they would drift in anywhere between 9:15 and 9:45. He tried to address this *effect* by docking their pay, rather than getting to the cause, and he got minimal results. A few people came in a little earlier, but many people seemed willing to lose money rather than toe the line for John. When he examined his thinking around this situation, John discovered he had a belief that "People don't support me." He worked hard to change this thinking and also addressed some underlying issues with his staff.

John changed his belief to, "People will work to support the team effort, to the degree that I support their interests and abilities." He began involving his employees in the vision he had for the company and for them. He also began to support them by acquiring the resources they needed to succeed. Within a couple months, everyone was operating as a team again.

Think of cause and effect as a movie and a television. Imagine that you rented a movie and it was terrible. You just hated it! Would you take a hammer and smash in your television screen, or would you change the movie? If you smashed in the screen, you would be dealing with effect. If you changed the movie, you would be dealing with cause.

"Many people are anxious to improve their results," James Allen says in *As A Man Thinketh*, "but are unwilling to improve themselves. They therefore remain bound." If we want to change our results, we have to change ourselves. We have to change the video, rather than smashing the television. When we change the cause, we change the effect. When we change our thought, we change our result.

The Science of Success is based on the premise that you have the power to shift your own mindsets. You can direct your inner powers of thought and free will to change your mindsets and to achieve whatever results you choose. To activate this power, we need to understand how the mind works, how mindsets are formed, and how they can be changed.

Let's begin by examining the mind.

YOUR MARVELOUS MIND

We all know that the mind is not the brain. We have Einstein's brain in a jar, and it isn't doing a thing. The brain is simply an instrument of the mind, the vehicle through which the mind works. But how does the mind work?

We human beings think in pictures, so in order to understand the mind, we need an accurate image of it. In the Science of Success, we understand that the mind has three compartments. Science tells us that the mind is omnipresent within us, as much present in our big toe as it is in our head. So the mind, as we will describe it here, is present in all three parts: the body, the conscious mind, and the unconscious mind. Actually, we know that the mind extends even beyond the body. But in this chapter, we will just look at these three parts of ourselves.

When fully understood, your mind will reveal to you a magnificent world of power, promise, and unlimited possibility. It can help you achieve whatever you want in your life, as it has for me. When I fully learned and understood the mind, I tripled a very good income in one year.

YOUR BODY

Your body is the most visible and obvious part of you, the part of you that moves around on the physical plane. But it is actually the least significant part of you. It is simply the vehicle you ride around in, a material instrument of the mind.

I'm not suggesting that our bodies aren't important. They are, and we should take good care of them. We need them in order to make things happen on the physical plane and to produce results. But we are much more than just our bodies. Philosopher Pierre Teilhard de Chardin said, "We are not physical beings having a spiritual experience; we are spiritual beings having a physical experience."

You and I have a power within us that is superior to any physical condition or circumstance around us, and we can direct this power to achieve whatever we want in life.

YOUR CONSCIOUS MIND

The conscious mind is the part of you that thinks and reasons. It is the repository of information from your five senses: smell, taste, sight, touch, and hearing. It also houses your six intellectual factors: memory, reason, will, intuition, imagination, and perception.

The most important thing for us to know about the conscious mind is that *we can choose our own thoughts.* Through our mind, we can accept or reject any idea. No person or situation can make you think thoughts or consider ideas that you do not choose to entertain. If you are entertaining two possibilities – for instance, that the glass is half empty, or that it is half full – you can consciously select one or the other as your reality. Through the power of the will, you are able to focus on the thoughts of your choosing, to the exclusion of other thoughts.

The thoughts you choose create impulses of energy that vibrate all through your body and beyond, and eventually determine your results in life.

One of the greatest examples of choosing thoughts is the story of Viktor Frankl. Frankl was a prisoner in Auschwitz, the Nazi concentration camp. In his book, *Man's Search for Meaning*, he recalls the enormous pain and injustice to which he was subjected while there. At one point, he was lying on an operating table, undergoing sterilization surgery with no anesthesia. The pain was unbearable, so Frankl began doing whatever he could to escape it in his mind.

He thought about the enormous difference between "liberty" and "freedom." Liberty was having an abundance of choices in your environment, the ability to come and go at will and to do whatever you pleased. Freedom was simply the ability to choose.

Frankl realized that, although his pain was excruciating and he had no liberty, he actually had more freedom than the men who were operating on him. He could say to himself, "I exercise my freedom to choose my thoughts and emotions. I choose to pity those men rather than to hate them." The men who were operating had many liberties, but they had given away their freedom, the freedom not to perform these inhuman acts on other human beings. They had to believe that "the system" was making them perform these acts and that they had no choice in the matter.

If Viktor Frankl could choose his thoughts under those extreme circumstances, we can certainly choose our thoughts in any situation we might find ourselves.

The idea that we can choose our own thoughts isn't always a popular idea. Many people would rather put the blame on others for "forcing" them to think certain things, or on circumstances that "caused" them to think in certain ways. But in the end, it's a fact that we can and do choose our own thoughts. And the thoughts we choose determine our results.

YOUR UNCONSCIOUS MIND

Your unconscious mind is your power center, the most magnificent part of you. It is the spiritual side of us, and some people even call it "spirit." The unconscious mind expresses itself through feelings and intuitions. It has no limits except those placed on it by your conscious mind as it chooses thoughts or by your previous conditioning. It is the greatest gift you have, a treasure chest of vast potential.

Your unconscious mind functions in every cell of your body. Try this experiment: Move your right arm in a circle. As you do so, think about the fact that it is your *unconscious* mind that carries out this order. There is no way that you could move approximately 157 muscles between your shoulder blade and your wrist *consciously*. That's just too much for your conscious mind to orchestrate. It's too complicated to say, "Well, let's rotate muscle #63 ten degrees to the right, muscle #32 eleven degrees to the left, etc."

Your unconscious mind simply receives the direction, "Move your right arm in a circle" and carries it out, much as it keeps your heart beating and your lungs breathing even while you sleep. Your conscious mind gave the command to move the arm, but the unconscious mind carried it out.

This process happens thousands, perhaps hundreds of thousands, of times each day. Every time your conscious mind entertains a thought, your unconscious mind begins to carry it out and manifest it in the world around you. This is why it's so important to choose your thoughts carefully. Whatever is held in the conscious mind goes right through to the unconscious and starts moving the body and invisible forces into action.

The unconscious mind has no ability to censor or reject information. It takes immediate action on whatever it is given. The unconscious mind cannot tell the difference between something that actually happened and something vividly imagined.

Any thought that you continuously impress upon your unconscious mind becomes fixed and habituated. *These fixed ideas and habits become your mindset. Our mindsets reside in the unconscious mind.* They continue to express themselves and to drive our results without any conscious assistance until they are deliberately replaced. Many times, we are not even aware of what they are, but they are active within our unconscious mind and they dictate our level of success until we consciously replace them.

The unconscious mind and the conscious mind are like a garden and a gardener. Your conscious mind is the gardener. You can use it to choose what seeds, or thoughts, you want to plant. Your unconscious mind will grow those seeds and produce results that exactly reflect the kinds of thoughts you planted. Whatever thoughts you accept and nurture will be grown in the garden and carried out by your unconscious mind.

THE PATH TO RESULTS

Here's how it works. We choose a thought in the conscious mind and get emotionally involved with it. As we continue to choose that thought and impress it upon the unconscious mind, the unconscious starts moving the body into action. That's exactly what happened a few minutes ago when you moved your arm. You consciously choose that thought and felt you wanted to do it. You gave the command and impressed it upon your unconscious, which activated all the muscles necessary to move your arm. That's how all results are created. Thoughts create feelings in your unconscious mind. Feelings create actions, and actions create results.

Change your thinking, and you change your results. Every thought you continuously think eventually winds up in physical form. If your thoughts change, your results must change.

THOUGHTS ⇨ FEELINGS ⇨ ACTIONS = RESULTS

HOW WE GET OUR MINDSETS

Our mindsets literally create our lives. If we believe, consciously or unconsciously, that vibrant good health is our birthright, then we are likely to have good health. If we believe that money is hard to come by and hard to keep, then that reality will manifest in our lives.

Where do we get these mindsets that cause us to think, feel, and act in a certain way toward ourselves, others, and our surroundings? Where do those original thoughts come from? Our mindsets are largely unsolicited gifts from our parents, teachers, religious sources, society, and other authorities. For the most part, you and I are the products of *other people's habitual ways of thinking.*

If my grandfather held the belief that money was "easy come, easy go," he may well have passed that mindset on to my father, who probably passed it on to me. Not one word about money may have passed between them, or between my father and me, but the message can be delivered in a million silent ways, every day, without any of us even being aware of what the message was or the fact that it was being delivered!

Our "outside sources" for mindsets don't have to sit us down and lecture us on their beliefs. They may not even be aware of them themselves! They simply live out these mindsets. We watch them and assume that's just how life is. We absorb their mindsets whether or not we are aware of what those mindsets are and whether or not we know we are absorbing them.

When we uncritically accept these values, beliefs, habits, or expectations and act on them, they gain control of our lives. They can produce positive, even outstanding, results. But they can also produce limiting, unwanted, ineffective, and even harmful results. Remember, we form our mindsets, and then our mindsets form us. To get different results, we have to rethink our thinking.

Consider these questions:

- Who has influenced my thinking about myself, about others, about life, and about success?
- What beliefs, attitudes, and habits of thought have they passed down to me?
- What societal attitudes, religious beliefs, or teachings are part of my mindset?
- Are these thoughts, attitudes, beliefs, and teachings enhancing my success or limiting it?

This last question is very important: How has your mindset limited or enhanced your success? What have you gained or lost as a result of it?

And even more importantly: *What can you do about your old mindset, the habits, practices, attitudes, values, beliefs, and expectations that limit what you create in your life?*

HOW TO CHANGE YOUR MINDSET

How can you change your mindset? To get rid of old, limiting programming, we have to constantly and consistently put new ideas into our minds. New ideas create positive, powerful new mindsets. Vincent van Gogh said, "I dream my painting, and then I paint my dream."

The key to creating a new mindset is *consistency.* Thinking new thoughts once in a while doesn't do much good. Meditating on your new mindset once or twice a day is fairly ineffective if the rest of your day is taken up with thoughts of fear or doubt.

It is the habitual thoughts, the consistent thoughts, that create your mindset and your destiny, not the thoughts that come and go. The thoughts you consistently and continually plant into your unconscious become *conviction* in your life. You can use affirmation and meditation to do this, but making your new mindset a habit also takes discipline, commitment, and resolve. This is why the power of the will in your conscious mind is one of your greatest gifts. If you catch yourself in the middle of negative thinking, stop and say "no" to those thoughts. Stop the thought and replace it with a positive one. Either mentally or verbally, say "Cancel" and repeat your new thought. As Nike says, "Just do it."

CREATING NEW PATHWAYS

Changing a mindset means pioneering a new way of life and carving a new trail for yourself. But the power we derive from this process and the results it produces are well worth the effort.

Imagine yourself at the edge of a dense jungle. Ahead of you, you see an old, well-worn path through the thick vegetation. It's tempting. It seems much easier just to start along that path than to cut a new path through the underbrush. All of nature tends to take the path of least resistance. A meandering stream goes *around* rocks, not *through* them. In the same way, you and I are more likely to take the well-worn path, the path of least resistance.

Your current mindset is like the well-worn path. It is a route you have taken before, and it was most likely formed by others around you. To form your own new mindset, you have to plunge into the jungle and start cutting a new path. At first, that may be difficult. You have to disrupt the jungle growth and stay committed to your new route even when it would be easier to return to the old path. It may be so hard that you start thinking, "This is too difficult. Why can't I just go back to the old way? It's much more comfortable."

Yet with discipline, perseverance, vision, and will, your new path begins to take shape. If you commit to traveling only on your new path, and if you travel it several times a day, every day, then it begins to get more comfortable. It becomes better defined. There is less resistance each time you travel it. You have developed your own route through life. *And it takes you exactly where you want to go,* not just where everyone else has gone before.

Soon your new path becomes much easier to travel. And the old path actually looks more difficult. Roots and plants have begun to grow over it, because you haven't been using it. Others may even see your new path and choose it for themselves, so that your new path continues to grow and becomes increasingly easier and more comfortable to walk. Eventually, your new mindset becomes so familiar that it is actually easier than the old one and guarantees you much better results.

The Science of Success depends on your willingness to create and think new thoughts, to carve a new path for yourself that leads to success.

You can't carve that new path through the jungle in one day. It takes time to build new habits in your unconscious mind. But as soon as your new convictions become deeper and stronger than the old ones, you will see results.

To change our lives, we must cut that new path. Here are some reminders as you begin the journey:

1. Resolve to keep your thoughts out of the old negative, limiting "path" and hold strongly to your new and positive thoughts

under any and all circumstances.

2. Make your new mindset as clear, strong, deep, and positive as possible.

3. Travel over your new "path" as frequently as you can.

4. Strengthen your new "path" with the power of emotions, faith, belief, conviction, and determination.

THE CLEAR GLASS OF WATER

Creating a new mindset is not brainwashing. It is simply giving our new, positive thoughts more attention and nurturing than we give our old, limiting thoughts.

Think of your mind as a glass full of cranberry juice. The cranberry juice represents old programming, and your goal is to have a mind full of crystal clear water, or new programming.

You might think the best way to get the glass full of clean water is to pour out all the cranberry juice, wash the glass, and start over with pure, fresh water. Not true. Even if it were possible to empty our minds of all the old programming that quickly and easily, it would represent a real shock to our systems. And it would usually take the path of least resistance and re-fill with more of the same. It's far better and more effective to use a more gradual approach.

Imagine that we simply start pouring clear water into the glass. The water begins to dilute the cranberry juice even before we can see much physical evidence of that. We just keep pouring water into the glass until it begins to overflow. What happens? At first, we have a bit of pure water and a lot of cranberry juice. That's fine. We have faith that changes are taking place even before we can see them. As we continue to pour, the color of the cranberry juice gets lighter and lighter. Eventually, as we keep pouring, the glass is filled with nothing except pure, clear water.

In the same way, we don't have to destroy our old thoughts

to create a new mindset. We just need to keep pouring new ones into our unconscious. We simply withdraw our attention from the old thoughts and give all our energy to the new ones. Eventually, the old mindset begins to wither and disappear. Our new mindset grows larger and stronger. Ultimately, it is all that remains, just as pure, clean water is all that remains in the glass.

At some point, you may even start wondering why you did some of the things you used to do. They simply don't make sense anymore. You are involved in your new ways of thinking, which are now the easier, more natural way to operate in the world.

Creating a new mindset takes some practice, but it gets easier with experience. And the payoffs are dramatic. True masters in life are always on the lookout for areas in which their old thoughts are limiting them and are always willing to do the work necessary to replace those old thoughts with new ones. They are willing to discipline their thinking and to nurture the new mindset that will make them more successful until it becomes stronger than the old one.

You can't think old, limiting thoughts and attract complete success. And you can't continuously think new, unlimited thoughts and not attract complete success. It's the law. Your firmly planted new mindset sets in motion a magnetic force that attracts into your life everything that is harmonious with it.

HOW FAR CAN YOU GO?

Given where you are now, how much good can you create for yourself? How far can you go with your new mindset? How successful can you become? All things are possible in the mind. Successful people through the ages have understood and used this truth. Walt Disney said, "If you can dream it, you can achieve it."

Whatever you can imagine, you can have. If you can bring up the image of yourself as a billionaire, living in a beautiful home, driving a Rolls Royce, in the most fulfilling relationship imaginable, or whatever you want, then that is what you can have.

If you have a desire, the very fact that you have that desire means that you have the means to fulfill it. Everything in physical form was first a thought. The clothes you are wearing, the car you drive, the house you live in, this book – everything was first a thought in someone's mind.

CHOOSING YOUR NEW MINDSET

How do you come up with your new mindset? How do you choose new thoughts to replace your old, limiting ones? Here are some tips for creating your new mindset:

1. *Make your mindset as real, concrete, and comprehensive as possible.* That means writing it down exactly as you want it to be. What are the new beliefs you want to live by? What are the new attitudes or opinions you want to adopt? What new mental habits and patterns would it benefit you to incorporate into your life? What are your real values? What are the expectations that will lead you to success? Who do you want to be? When you read your new mindset and picture yourself living it, what does the picture look like? Where are you? How do you feel? What do you see? Who is around you? What would a typical day look like if you were living with those new attitudes, beliefs, and thoughts?

   Start by writing, "I am so happy, and grateful now that..." Then proceed to describe your beliefs, attitudes, opinions, mental habits, values, and expectations exactly as you want them to be.

2. *Think in an unlimited way.* Give yourself permission to envision yourself and your attitudes about yourself, others, and how the world works exactly as you would like them to be.

Remember our discussion in Chapter 1 about being worthy. Don't go for what you think you can get. Claim the life you really want!

3. *Be sure to use the present tense.* You must not think in terms of "someday," or write "I will be." Write it and experience it, as if it were true *right now,* even if the results have not yet manifested. Write, for instance, "I love making money and running a successful business, because it allows me to be generous to others." Give your unconscious mind the message that this reality is already manifest in your life.

   Remember, the unconscious mind accepts everything it is given, without editing, censoring, or judging. If you write in the future tense, it tells your unconscious mind that *you do not have what you want, and you are not yet the person you want to be.* When you say, "I will be," you are saying to your unconscious mind that you are *not.* I once read an organizational mission statement that said they were "striving to become number one." Guess what they were always doing. Striving! With that mission statement, they would always be striving, but never being, number one! If you catch yourself slipping into the future tense, go back and bring your mindset description back into the present.

4. *Make your mindset emotional.* In addition to writing in the present tense, include emotional words and get involved emotionally in what you are writing. Remember, feelings are the gateway to the unconscious mind, and your unconscious mind is the real power behind your success. Emotion creates motivation. You must get passionate. Unless you are passionate about your new mindset, unless you truly fall in love with it, it will not come into physical form. The human spirit will not invest itself in mediocrity! If you aren't excited after writing your

new mindset, then go back and rework what you have done. When it completely turns you on, you're ready to bring it into reality.

5. *Be careful to state what you do want, not what you don't want.* Our minds cannot process a negative. If I tell you not to think about an ice cream cone, what do you think about? You must first think of what I told you not to think about, before you can tell your mind not to think about it! All this thinking will cause you to attract the very thing you don't want. So remember to state what you do want.

6. *Create a picture of your mindset and be* **in** *the picture, not just an observer looking* **at** *it.* When I ask people to do this exercise, they almost always find that they are looking at themselves in the picture. This doesn't work. You must be *in* the picture of your new mindset. If you're looking *at* yourself in the picture, you're telling your unconscious that it's not really you, that you're not really there yet. When you're actually in the picture, you are experiencing the emotions and results that you already have in your new life. You are telling your unconscious, "This is real!" Your unconscious immediately goes about creating that reality. See what you would see if you were *in* the picture, not looking *at* yourself in the picture.

When you begin living from your new mindset, you start to make different decisions. You may begin to associate with different kinds of people, and you attract different circumstances into your life. The more frequently and passionately you bring your mindset into your mind, the more rapidly it will manifest.

These tips are effective whether you are working with a new mindset or with a new vision, as you will be doing in the next chapter.

Every single one of the Super Laws can be used to bring your dreams into reality. Begin by using the Law of Attraction. Live your new mindset as if it were here right now, and watch it take physical form in your life!

We know that the unconscious mind cannot distinguish between something that is "real" in material form and something that is vividly imagined. Because your mind thinks in pictures, you must create a mental picture of yourself living your new life mindset.

Remember, thoughts are powerful and the unconscious mind is their obedient servant. Like the genie in Aladdin's lamp, the unconscious mind says, "Your wish is my command." It begins to create whatever you think about, or worry about. Don't confuse it by staying on track one day and lapsing into doubt or negativity the next. Give the genie clear instructions, and you will soon be living your new mindset.

My friend Leslie shifted her mindset dramatically when she was diagnosed with terminal cancer. She began investigating the causes of cancer and alternative treatments and decided on a whole new mindset for herself that included no more drinking or smoking, a strict vegetarian diet, and a positive attitude that told her she would beat the odds. She began reading and listening to positive ideas that supported her new beliefs and decisions and continued to picture herself as already healthy and whole.

Leslie's life changed completely. She lost a few friends who couldn't understand her lack of interest in going to the bars, but a year and a half after her diagnosis, she had a complete remission without undergoing chemotherapy.

To shape your future, you have to be ready and able to shape your mindsets. In the next chapter, you'll learn to combine the Power of Mindsets with the power of a compelling vision to move you rapidly forward.

SUMMARY

CHAPTER 3: THE POWER OF MINDSETS

1. Your mindset is the sum total of all your beliefs, values, identity, expectations, attitudes, habits, decisions, opinions, and thought patterns about yourself, others, and how life works.

2. Many of our mindsets are handed down from our families, society, religious authorities, and teachers, but we can change our thoughts and mindsets to attract more of whatever it is we want.

3. The mind is composed of body, conscious mind, and unconscious mind. The conscious mind gives the order, and the unconscious mind carries it out through the body. To choose your new path, create a clear mental picture of your new mindset and give all your attention and energy to those new thoughts, attitudes, and beliefs. The old will wither and die.

THE POWER OF VISION

THE POWER OF MINDSETS SHOWS US THAT we can actually change our thoughts, beliefs, values, opinions, and attitudes to reflect the people we want to be and to attract the relationships, situations, and success that we want in our lives.

The third Power Principle, the Power of Vision, helps us create a clear mental picture of the life we want to live and start programming our thoughts to produce exactly the results we want.

As we have seen, there is one great law: Everything is energy. We also know through the Law of Attraction that similar vibrations attract, and dissimilar vibrations repel. Therefore, we attract to us people and circumstances that vibrate in *harmony* or *resonance* with our thoughts. To get what we want, we must plant those thoughts firmly in our mind. We must nurture them, give them attention, focus on them, and become them. We must align body, mind, and spirit with what we desire.

The first step in doing this is to define what you want with absolute clarity. The Bible says, "Where there is no vision, the people perish."

WHAT DO YOU WANT?

Most of us don't have what we want in our lives because we never really define precisely what that is. Left to our own devices, we just go along with our conditioning, accepting the mindsets and visions we inherited from our families, society, religions, and other authorities. Those old ideas, beliefs, and thought processes have been fixed in our unconscious minds, and we accept them without question. The result is that we create exactly those circumstances that we have accepted.

When we understand this process, we can change it. When we discover that our habits, mindsets, and visions are not to our benefit, we can replace them. We can escape the outcomes of our past conditioning and create our dreams.

Again, it's helpful to think of your unconscious mind as a garden. Your old habits, mindsets, and visions of life are like weeds. They grow on their own. You don't have to work to make them thrive. Even when you cover over the weeds with concrete, they grow through the cracks! But the beautiful flowers in your garden, your new unlimited mindset and vision, need love and care. They need to be fed, watered, touched, pampered, and protected from the weeds.

It's not enough to simply pull out the weeds, because nature abhors a vacuum. They will grow back if they are not replaced with new flowers, new truths. Old thinking must be constantly replaced with new thoughts to keep the garden of your life beautiful and healthy.

The best way to do this is to keep the vision of your new life clear and strong. Your vision takes you along an entirely new path. It keeps the weeds from growing back. You let go of the old and embrace your new life.

WHAT IS A VISION?

A vision is your mental picture of the life you want to lead. Clarity is power. To achieve the highest levels of success, create the highest vision you can dream and deposit it in the treasury of your unconscious mind.

Before we begin that process, I want to make the distinction between a vision and a goal. Goals are an important part of life, and they are necessary to move you forward. But a vision is not a goal. A vision is much broader and more compelling than a goal. It is a complete, overall picture of your life that includes both personal and professional endeavors.

Goals are *part* of your vision, the stepping stones that get you where you want to go. For example, Janet wanted to be a doctor. That vision included goals like graduating with honors from college, graduating from medical school, completing an internship, and opening a practice. Each of these goals was essential, and each helped keep her on track. But "being a doctor" was far more expansive and far more inspiring than "completing my internship," and "being a doctor" was only part of her larger vision that also included a family and a home in the country. That vision kept her heart bright and her emotions alive, even as her individual goals guided her steps.

Your vision determines what your goals are, and goals are milestones that mark your progress toward your vision. The vision will continue to pull and attract you long after individual goals are accomplished.

Only you can create your vision. Others in your life – your spouse, your parents, your siblings, your employer and colleagues – may offer suggestions, but *you* must make the final choices.

THE THREE LEVELS OF VISION

To create the highest vision for yourself, think about what you want on three levels:

- What you want to be
- What you want to do
- What you want to have

What we "have" and what we "do" are important, wonderful parts of our lives. But the only part of us that is changeless is the "be." It's great to have a beautiful home, take great vacations, and achieve other material goals, but we are only the temporary custodians of these possessions. We are enjoying them for a time, but who we are in our hearts goes on forever. You can and will create all the material success you want, but to experience the fullness of success, you must also create a "be" that is worthy of a child of Spirit. Life is not about what we have or what we do; it is about who we become. All lasting growth and change happen from the inside out. You can, and should, do and have whatever you desire, but always do things and have things to assist you in becoming more of who you truly are.

As you create your vision, start with the most important and powerful level: "be." Then move on to what you want to "do." Finally, explore what you want to "have" as a result. Johann Wolfgang Goethe said, "Before you can do something, you must first be something."

CREATING YOUR VISION

How do you start? The guidelines for writing down your vision are the same as those for creating your new mindset:

1. *Make your vision as real, concrete, and comprehensive as possible.* Create a picture that includes your physical, mental, emotional, and spiritual well-being. Find your own individual harmony between personal and professional. For some people, working 12-hour days is a good balance. For others, it is not. Be honest about what balance is good for you, and take into account all three levels of your vision: "be," "do," and "have." Life is meant to be fulfilling and complete in all areas.

It may help you to think about how you want to be remembered. What do you want people to say about you after you are gone? How do you want people to talk about you? Think of the good you can do for the people around you. Now, see yourself being that person. Feel what it's like to be that person. Become that person in your mind.

2. *Think in an unlimited way.* Let go of all limitations in your thinking, and just allow yourself to dream. Approach your vision knowing that you can have anything and everything that you desire. All things are possible through the power of spirit and your magnificent mind.

3. *Be sure to use the present tense.* You must be able to see yourself already living the good that you desire. Say, "I am a billionaire" rather than, "I will be a billionaire." Your billions may not have come to you yet, but this is what you're programming into your unconscious mind. If you tell your unconscious mind, "I will be a billionaire," you are not being a billionaire.

   If you say, "I wish for a new car," that's exactly what your unconscious mind will create for you: the *wish*, not the actuality. Instead, write, "I'm happy and excited driving my new Mercedes S-Class."

4. *Make your vision emotional.* Let emotion fuel your vision. The unconscious cannot distinguish between something that actually happens and something that is vividly imagined, so use vivid, colorful, emotional words to give your vision power.

5. *Be careful to state what you **do** want, not what you **don't** want.* If I tell you, "Don't think about an ice cream cone," what do you have to think of? You have to think about what not to think about in order not to think about it. If one of your goals is "to have no sick days," you'll have to think about sick days. It's better to think about being "continuously healthy."

6. *Be **in** the picture, not just an observer looking **at** it.* As I've said, when I ask people to do this exercise, they almost always find that they are looking *at* themselves in the picture. This doesn't work. You must be *in* the picture of your new vision. If you're looking at yourself in the picture, you're telling your unconscious that it's not really you, that you're not really in the picture yet. When you're actually in the picture, you already have your new life. You are telling your unconscious, "This is real!" Your unconscious immediately goes about creating that reality. See what you would see if you were *in* the picture, not looking *at* yourself in the picture.

WRITING IT DOWN

Now, take three large pieces of paper. At the top of one, write "What I Want To Be." Be sure to include the physical, mental, and spiritual aspects of what you want to be. Write for five minutes without letting your pen stop. Just keep it moving. Remember that everything is possible.

At the top of another piece of paper, write "What I Want To Do." Take another five minutes without letting your pen stop, and write down everything you ever want to do in life: physically, mentally, and spiritually.

At the top of a third piece of paper, write "What I Want To Have." Again, include the physical, mental, and spiritual aspects of what you want to have, and write for five minutes without letting your pen stop.

Don't worry about how you will be, do, or have these things. If your intention is clear and you are passionately involved in your vision, the means for achieving it will come to you. The how-to's will simply begin to manifest in ways more magnificent that you can imagine.

Are you excited about what you have written? Can you get emotionally involved in it? If so, great! If not, go back and rework your answers.

Next, go back to your "Be" page, your "Do" page, and your "Have" page, and count the number of items on each page. Then divide that number into thirds. If you have fifteen items on your "Be" page, for instance, you will have five, five, and five. If you have twelve items, you'll have four, four, and four.

When you know the number, go back and prioritize what you have written. Designate a third of your items on the "Be" page as most important and assign them an "A." Do the same with your "Do" and "Have" pages. Give a "B" to the third of those items on each of the pages that are slightly less important and a "C" to those items that are least important on each page. If you have fifteen items on each page, then five of them will be "As," five of them will be "Bs," and five of them will be "Cs."

When you have finished doing this, go back and number all of your "As" in order of priority, with #1 being the most important, #2 being the next important, etc. Ask yourself, "If I could have only one of these items, which one would it be?" Assign "1" to that item. Then ask yourself, "If I could have only one more, which one would it be?" Get all of your "A" items in numerical order.

Repeat this process for your "Do" and "Have" pages.

When you are finished, you will have three goals that are "A1." One will be a "Be," one will be a "Do," and one will be a "Have." These are the three most important things in your life. What can you do to bring them closer to you? Take a clean piece of paper and write down one thing that you will do within the next twenty-four hours to move yourself closer to your vision.

If part of your vision is to be financially independent, for instance, you can go to the bank and open a new savings account, even if it only has $5 in it. If part of your vision is to be a great parent, you can schedule a day with your son or daughter. If you want to go on a cruise around the world, you can call the travel agent and get a brochure. If there is a new car in your vision, you can go down to a showroom and sit in it. The thing you do to move closer to your vision doesn't have to be anything huge, but it does have to be something to which you can absolutely commit to doing within the next twenty-four hours.

USE EMOTION AS FUEL

Emotion is the fuel that carries your vision into physical reality. You will only succeed with a vision that fills you with passion. I cannot emphasize enough how crucial emotional energy is to the success of your vision. The only way to make your vision real is to fall in love with it. A vision that succeeds is a vision that is *compelling*.

Jim Webb had a vision of driving in the Indianapolis 500 race for thirty-three years. He wrote to a friend of mine recently, "I know that in the past, I was thinking in reverse. I thought I needed the money before I could prepare for the race." After he started studying what I call the Power of Vision, he got up every morning and went over his vision and goals. He saw himself racing each lap, qualifying, and winning the Indy 500. He pictured himself with the prizes and the winning check made out for $1.6 million. He started talking to companies about sponsoring his team. At the end of the day, he again relaxed and went over his vision. "Long story short," he wrote, "after using the visualization techniques, I am excited to say that I am racing in the 1997 Indianapolis 500."

Emotion drives us into action. If you don't believe that, look at the watch on your wrist. If you paid more than $40 for that watch, you made an emotional purchase. A $40 watch will tell time just as well as a $4,000 watch. If you paid more than $40, you did so because of how that watch would make you *feel*.

Some people say, "But wait, I'm a very reasonable, rational, logical person. I don't make decisions based on emotion." I believe that even if you are reasonable and rational, you make decisions based on how *strongly* you feel something is reasonable or rational. You don't have to be enveloped in some of the more obvious emotions – love, hate, sadness, joy – in order to make emotional decisions.

Emotion is our greatest motivator. It is our spirit speaking to us and wanting to come forward. Every thought that you mix with emotion becomes a seed that you plant in your unconscious mind. That seed will grow to the extent that it is nourished with repetition, faith, and belief.

THE POWER OF FAITH AND BELIEF

Napoleon Hill said, "There is a difference between wishing for a thing... and being ready to receive it." No one is ready for a thing until they believe they can acquire it. Before anything can come to us, we have to envision it and believe that it is ours.

Many individuals have written out their visions, just as you did, and never achieved anything. Why did others succeed, when they did not? What makes the difference? Why are some people incredibly successful, while others continue to struggle and never really succeed? It's not that there is some higher power playing favorites, reaching down and touching a select few. Often, the people who succeed are those with the strongest faith.

Unbending belief and unshakable faith are the essential elements of bringing your vision into physical reality. All great achievers have an absolute belief that their visions will manifest. They know without any doubt that their dreams will come to them. These people don't waste time having faith one minute and then allowing themselves to sink back into fear or doubt the next. That would only attract confusion and anxiety. Great achievers focus only on their visions and fire those visions with faith, regardless of their current circumstances. They know that it is only a matter of time before their visions manifest in physical form.

"To believe in the things you can see and can touch is no belief at all," Abraham Lincoln said, "but to believe in the unseen is both a triumph and a blessing."

Faith and belief not only act as powerful agents in achieving our dreams, but they keep us centered, calm, and present to ourselves and our lives. When we have faith and belief that our dreams are coming to us, we never hurry. Hurry is a manifestation of fear. Fear is based on doubt and lack of belief. Fear, doubt, and lack of belief are based on an ignorance of the truth that we are all one with Supreme Intelligence.

The Law of Gender says that your goodness will come to you in the correct fashion and in the correct time. This Super Law governs creation, and you are creating success. It states that every "new" thing comes into being because different existing energies have united, and that everything has its own incubation or gestation period. When we have faith, we don't try to hurry along our dreams before they are ready to come to fruition any more than we hurry a baby to be born before nine months have elapsed. Faith gives us patience with our visions and dreams. Success is coming. It already exists and is just waiting for you to attract it.

Don't cut yourself off from this creative flow with self-doubts, limiting beliefs, or lack of understanding. The only thing that can go wrong is your thinking. When you find yourself beginning to hurry or worry, stop! The minute you act in haste, you disconnect from Supreme Intelligence and will not receive the power and wisdom that are rightfully yours. Re-affirm that you are one with the source of all that exists. Your belief will never waver if you stay connected with the truth of who you are. Listen for the "still, small voice" of your intuition to tell you what to do

When you get the message, then *act*! Don't worry about what others think. They are probably far more interested in what people are thinking about *them* than they are in judging *you*. Until you perfect your intuitive abilities, you may make some "mistakes." You may misjudge an impulsive urge to buy a car as the voice of supreme intelligence within you, but you will gradually build your "intuitive muscle." You will learn how to listen and act in faith and belief. You will recognize the "still, small voice" when you hear it, and you will develop the courage to trust and follow it every time.

When you act in complete faith and confidence while listening to your internal wisdom, everything will unfold according to divine order, exactly when and as it should: never too early or too late. Whatever assistance, resources, or relationships you may need will come to you exactly when they are needed. Whatever wisdom or knowledge you need is also seeking you. Even if you don't know which way to turn next, you will be handed the book you need, meet the person you need to meet, or manifest the money necessary to accomplish your dreams, and it always happens at the perfect time.

Again, we can look to the mind to understand how this principle works. At the intellectual or conscious level, your vision must *be here now*, in the present tense. You must visualize yourself in the picture and look out through your own eyes from within your vision. At the unconscious or spiritual level, your vision must also be here and now. Do this by using your emotions. Get emotionally involved in your vision. Get passionate about it. Remember, the human spirit will not invest in mediocrity. At the physical level, your vision has no choice but to begin manifesting.

VISUALIZING YOUR VISION

Science has proven the power of visualization, and its ability to create. Golfer Jack Nicholas always visualizes his stroke before he hits the ball. He feels his swing and sees the ball flying exactly where he wants it to go before each shot. Michael Jordan always runs through the entire game in his mind before he ever leaves the locker room. Every shot, every move, every pass is a mental image before it becomes a physical reality. When great gymnasts are injured, they are told to practice by lying on the mat and visualizing their performance.

Manifest your vision the same way you manifest your new mindset: by using your willpower to focus on it exclusively and with laser-like intensity. The more frequently you do so, the more quickly it will manifest.

First, take your three "A1" vision components and create a picture around them. You may want to incorporate elements of the mindset you created in the last chapter and build one big picture that includes both your mindset and your vision.

Visualize yourself actually living within this image at least once a day. Find a quiet time to do the exercise I'm about to describe to you. Remember, your unconscious never sleeps. *The last thought you think each night before drifting off to sleep is what you give your unconscious mind to work with all night long*, so the best time to visualize your vision is right before you go to sleep each night.

First, let yourself relax as your head sinks into the pillow. Begin to feel yourself living your vision. Make it colorful and emotional. Be within the picture, not as an observer but as an active participant. Imagine yourself walking, talking, and feeling as if you already have your vision in physical form. Hear the sounds, feel the emotions, smell the smells, touch the textures, and see the sights. Then hold that picture as you drift off to sleep. Your unconscious mind will take it and begin to work with it all night. That vibration will be sent out and the Law of Attraction will begin to bring those results into your life.

If you want more rapid results, practice this visualization when you first wake up as well. If you want your vision even more quickly, add a visualization around mid-day. Wherever you are, just let yourself relax. Begin to see, hear, and feel yourself in your vision. Bring up your picture and run the tape all the way though. Make it bigger, better, brighter, and more fun each time you see it. Let your feelings become more intense. The more vividly and frequently you imagine your vision, the more quickly it will come to you.

Take action toward your vision each day. Walk, talk, and think as if it were already yours. Do not concern yourself with tomorrow. Give 100% to every action today that will move you toward your vision.

SUMMARY
CHAPTER 4: THE POWER OF VISION

1. To create the life of your dreams, create a clear, precise vision that includes "Be," "Do," and "Have."

2. Fire your vision with emotion, faith, and belief.

3. Make sure that you are in the picture, looking through your own eyes.

4. Visualize it as frequently and vividly as possible, and it must come to you.

5. Take immediate action each day to move you toward your vision.

6. Act "as if" it has already occurred. Strengthen your belief and faith in yourself and your vision.

THE POWER OF
PARTNERSHIPS

*"Men take on the nature, the habits, and the power
of thought of those with whom they associate."*
NAPOLEON HILL

WE LIVE IN A WORLD THAT IS ON FAST-FORWARD, and in the midst of
an information explosion. Each year, we are expected to produce
more, more quickly, using fewer resources. To break even, let alone
succeed, we must leverage ourselves. We must find ways of multi-
plying, maximizing, and synergizing the energy available to us. The
key to thriving in this new world is *powerful partnerships.*

Anyone who tells you that they are succeeding by themselves
today is not being honest. Even people who work very smart and
very hard find it extremely difficult to keep up if they work by
themselves. Partnerships are vital to the Science of Success. The
next step after creating your own new mindset and clearly defining
your vision is to leverage your time, talents, and actions through the
fourth Power Principle, the Power of Partnerships.

NETWORKING: LITTLE THINGS MEAN EVERYTHING

It's often said that in five years we will be the sum total of who we
are today plus four other elements: the books we read, the tapes we
listen to, the seminars we attend, and the people with whom we
spend our time. I believe that. I read recently that 70% of new jobs
are obtained through networking, and I believe this figure is even
higher for creating new business opportunities.

I fly frequently in my work, and I always make a point of meeting the person next to me and learning something about him or her. When I get home, I send a hand-written note thanking them for their time and conversation.

I recently sat next to a Vice President of Sales for a Fortune 500 company. We talked about sales in general and about the Science of Success, and I wrote him my usual note. Two weeks later, he called and we talked more about my work. After a few conversations, I signed a contract for multiple speaking engagements with his company. Over dinner at the first of these events, he told me that he had called because he was intrigued by my ideas, but mostly because he was impressed that I had written him the note.

We always hear that "little things mean a lot." I believe they mean everything! In this case, a genuine interest in a person and his business, a stimulating conversation, and a small courtesy resulted in a pleasant and profitable partnership.

CREATION OR COMPETITION?

Why don't more people build powerful partnerships today? Doesn't it make sense that you leverage your power when you build partnerships with supportive, powerful people? And that you increase your success while minimizing the effort it takes to achieve what you want? I believe that part of the answer is that we are conditioned to compete with one another.

One of the most striking facts that my research revealed is that *truly successful people never compete.* The reason successful people avoid competition is that when you compete, you limit yourself and restrict your ability to create. Consider the kinds of thoughts that must be created for competition. You must:

1. Compare yourself to your "adversary," and think that someone will win and the other must lose.

2. Believe that there is a limited supply of goodness and success.

Both of these thoughts are in error, and completely out of alignment with the Super Laws. Let's look at them one at a time.

First, it's important to understand that we have no external adversaries. Your success, or lack of it, comes directly from your own thoughts. Other people have no power to keep you from your good. So *the only real competition you will ever have in life is the competition between the positive thoughts of your disciplined mind and the negative thoughts of your undisciplined mind*. You are only in competition with you. If you must have an adversary, let that adversary be lack of understanding. That is the only thing that will slow your success.

If you want to win against that undisciplined part of you, the part that doesn't understand the laws, then read this book over and over. Do the exercises again and again until you lock them into your spiritual power center. Make the magnetic attraction between your thoughts and your good absolutely clear, unshakable, and irresistible.

Not competing is just the first step in building successful partnerships. I believe that we must go a step farther. I believe we must have a genuine interest in people and a real desire for their success as well as our own. That generosity of spirit is worth developing if it isn't already in place. It's good for others, good for the world, and especially good for you. It will draw your good to you even more quickly.

To counter the second competitive assumption, that there is a limited supply of goodness and success, keep in mind that there is no such thing as a limited supply. Remember, the Super Laws tell us that nothing is ever created or destroyed. All that ever *was* is and ever shall be. This is the law. The marketplace is full of people and companies doing the same kind of business, providing similar services, and yet many of them prosper. Your "competition" can earn millions of dollars, and there will still be millions left for you. Their success has no effect on yours!

This is radical thinking, but it is absolutely accurate. It follows the laws. It's not the collective consciousness, but often the way to succeed is to see which way the masses are heading, and walk in the other direction.

Highly successful people do not compete; they *create*. They discipline their thoughts to focus not on other people, but on their own results: on the success they are creating and on the abundant possibilities available to them.

Whenever we let our thoughts drift to comparing ourselves with others, we are doomed to create nothing more than those people's best efforts. If that's what we think about, that's what we create. If we're thinking about our own new mindsets and visions, then *that's* what we create. If you truly want to succeed, resolve now, once and for all, to concentrate only on what you want and on the abundance of possibility available to you.

STARBUCKS' SUCCESS: A STUDY IN CREATING

Starbucks Coffee is a classic American success story, and it is built on the idea of creating, rather than competing. In 1982, Starbucks CEO Howard Schultz left his $75,000 job at Xerox to pursue his entrepreneurial dream. He never saw himself as competing with the existing coffee market, which was actually in a state of decline with rising interest in teas, price wars, and poor quality products. Instead, Schultz developed a new mindset for coffee, gourmet coffees, and created a whole new market. He didn't react to the existing market; he filled a niche that others didn't even see as a possibility.

The results were staggering! Starbucks grew from approximately six stores and less than 100 employees in 1987 to more than 1,300 stores and 25,000 employees in 1997. Sales and profits grew by more than 50% a year for six consecutive years, and they hired more than 500 new employees each month.

When I used to drink coffee, I gladly stood in line to pay $5 for my cup of Starbucks coffee! I doubt if anyone ever thought it would be a great idea to pay $5 for a cup of gourmet coffee, but the gourmet coffee business is booming. By creating, not competing, Howard Schultz developed an entire new industry, demonstrating further proof that competition has no impact on success.

CHOOSING YOUR PARTNERSHIPS

When you give up competition, you are also liberated from petty arguments and free to be the very best you can be, for yourself and for the people around you. When you know in your heart that no one can keep you from your own success, you automatically start to help others. When people help and support one another, everybody wins. Everybody gets more than they would have gotten by working alone.

The more you help others, the more you attract that same energy to you. Focusing on your new mindset and vision will draw people to you who are in harmony with the *person you are becoming* and the *direction you are moving.* These will be people who believe in you and support the reality that you are creating. They will start helping you achieve your goals. Their support will energize your vision and help you manifest it even more quickly. You will start building partnerships. Now the question becomes, "How do you choose the right partners?"

This is my best advice about choosing partners: *Commit to building intimate relationships only with people you would want to become.* I made this commitment about six years ago, and it changed my life. I had to let go of some friendships and start hanging out with different people. It made all the difference in the world. This doesn't mean that you won't see your current friends and acquaintances. It just means that your intimate relationships will be only with people whom you admire and people you would want to become.

If you don't want to be like someone, don't invest heavily in the relationship, whether it is personal or professional. Eagles don't fly with pigeons! This is a simple, blunt example, but it makes the point. Eagles and pigeons have entirely different vibrations. They repel, rather than attract, one another.

Unless you are very unusual, you probably have people in your life right now who are limiting you. I have seen many, many potential high achievers limit themselves with disempowering relationships. Some of the people who are currently in your life may not understand what you are creating. Even those who love you the most may, with good intentions, tell you to "slow down," "take your time," or "be realistic." They may have your best interest at heart, but this kind of thinking will hold you back nevertheless.

Other people may be true nay-sayers, and give you every reason in the world why you cannot achieve your vision. These people may be very close to you, but they are toxic. To many of them, you may represent the courage they don't have and the person they are unwilling to become. Guard yourself, your vision, and your emotions when you are in their presence. This doesn't mean they can't be in your life, but be aware that they are dangerous to your dreams.

On the road to success, you may have to make some changes. You may have to realign some of your relationships and even start spending time in different places, but the rewards are enormous. You will find new friends and have new places to go. If you hold yourself to the highest standards, the people and places in your life will begin to reflect those new standards. Successful people invariably spend quality time with other successful people. They join the same clubs and churches, attend the same functions, and even eat at the same restaurants.

You can't afford to be casual about your partners and relationships. They have an enormous influence on your success. You need to take them very seriously and to approach them with your vision in mind. People are the portals through which we pass into positions of power and leadership.

PARTNER POWER

All things are possible to you, especially when you have the right partners. A couple I know became infatuated with an expensive home while they were on vacation in Phoenix. It cost several million dollars and they knew they couldn't qualify for the loan. Not discouraged, they moved forward in faith and in the strength of their partnership.

They mind-stormed with friends about how to purchase this dream home. Eventually, they devised a plan to raise money for the down payment through their network of partners whom they could pay back when they got the cash from a deal that would close a few months down the line. They got their dream home, but that was just the beginning of what they accomplished through their network.

This couple believed they were one another's soulmates, and they wanted to share that idea with people. They had another mind-storming session with friends, and one of their partners said that they should title the book *Chicken Soup for Soulmates*. Things took off and before they knew it, they were discussing the idea with the authors of the wildly successful *Chicken Soup for the Soul*.

Their book is being published under a different *Chicken Soup* title, and they have seen once again that partners are the most valuable asset you can have. It's not always just who you know, but who your *partners* know.

We all need to see and touch greatness in other people. We need to be around people who believe in us, inspire us, and motivate us toward our visions.

In seminars, I often suggest that people answer a series of questions to start getting clear about the kinds of individuals they want to draw into their lives and the kinds of relationships they want to nurture and develop. The questions for business and social partnerships are similar, but slightly different. Take some time to see which relationships you want to cultivate. Then look at what you will do to deepen those relationships.

CHOOSING YOUR BUSINESS PARTNERSHIPS

- List the people with whom you currently spend most of your business time.
- From this list and others not on your current list, who do you aspire to be like?
- Which of these relationships would you like to cultivate?
- What specifically will you do to create or deepen these relationships? By what date?
- What will you do to help these people? Give them a specific business idea? A referral?

CHOOSING YOUR SOCIAL PARTNERSHIPS

- List the people with whom you currently socialize. With whom do you go to movies or dinner?
- From this list and others not on your list, who do you aspire to become?
- Which of these relationships would you like to cultivate? If all the people on your list are just like you, consider bringing

in someone of a different race, gender, religion, industry, or neighborhood.

- What, specifically, will you do to create or deepen these relationships? By what date?
- What will you do to help these people? By when?

MENTORS

Mentors are people who have already achieved a level of success to which you aspire, and to whom you can go for guidance and insight. Having a mentor is one of the most powerful partnerships you can create. You will increase both the level and the speed of your success by working with a great mentor. All highly successful individuals have had powerful teachers.

I've had mentors since I was very young, and they have been some of the most powerful and significant forces in my life. They have shortened my learning curve exponentially, and I believe that finding a mentor is one of the best things you can do for yourself and your success. You can make it without a mentor, but it may take twice the time and effort.

Mentors have been where you are going. They know what works and doesn't work. They can tell you from experience what to do and what not to do. They have made the mistakes and stepped in the potholes, so they can tell you how to avoid trouble.

Here are some questions that can help you choose a great mentor:

- List people whom you want to meet and emulate. Who are the experts in your field? Who has the Harmonic Wealth you'd like to attain? Who would you like to learn parenting tips from? List six people who have achieved what you want to achieve in various areas of life. Select two or three who could actually be your mentor.

- What needs to happen for you to meet these people? Who do you know who knows them? It's often said that we are, at most, only five people away from anyone in the world. Who could help you meet this person? Whom can you call? What immediate action can you commit to taking toward meeting these people? By what specific date?

- What can you do to build a relationship with your future mentor(s)? By when will you do this?

You now have some excellent people on your list for business partnerships, social relationships, and mentoring. You've made some important commitments to yourself. What next?

To establish the relationship you want with these people, you must be able to communicate with them effectively. In every area of life, the thing that makes you most successful is being a master communicator.

BECOMING A MASTER COMMUNICATOR

Life is about relationships. According to the Law of Relativity, nothing is real until we relate it to something else. No matter what the arena – business, committees, organizations, social partnerships, neighborhood associations, romantic relationships, or family connections – everything is driven by how we relate to other people.

Relationships are built on rapport, which means being in the same vibration as another person. To build effective partnerships, we must be able to establish rapport as quickly as possible. Rapport is made up of communication, commonality, and connection. We need to be able to get our message across clearly, we must have something in common with the other person, and we need to reach out and touch them in some way.

When we are in rapport with someone, we communicate on three levels: physical, intellectual, and spiritual. This happens whether the relationship is personal or professional and whether it is in sales, leadership, finance, or standing over the backyard fence. Let's look at each of these three levels of communication.

The *intellect*, or *conscious mind*, communicates through words, gestures, and writing. To the degree that you establish commonality in these ways, you establish rapport. You both begin to think, "This person is like me." This opens the door to deeper levels of communication.

Here's how it works. Think for a moment about how it feels to be around your best friends, family members, and business associates. Are there certain words that you and these people use regularly? Is there a certain way you say things to one another or a certain tone that you use? Are there gestures that you use often that are almost like a code? Have you ever noticed yourself talking the same way someone else talks when you have been around them for awhile? Do you have little code names or jokes? Do you pick up one another's slang words? These are the kinds of things that happen when we are in rapport at the conscious level.

The next time you are in a restaurant, notice how people at the tables around you are talking to one another. Some are obviously connected with one another, in deep rapport. They will be sitting in a similar way, making similar gestures, and probably talking at about the same volume and speed.

You can consciously deepen your rapport with other people by mirroring their key words, voice tone, and gestures. For instance, if the person with whom you are interacting speaks very softly and slowly, you probably would *not* build rapport by talking very quickly and loudly. This isn't manipulation. Your intention is to build a relationship, and you are establishing rapport in order to create positive energy with another human being. We use these techniques to connect with other people all the time. Master communicators just use them more consciously, quickly, and effectively.

The *unconscious* level of rapport works through vibration and emotion. This is the level of feelings. Sometimes you may not be able to explain exactly why you like another person; it's just a feeling or sense that you have. You are comfortable around the person and your guard is down. When this bond is established, you develop a deep trust for one another. Your unconscious minds are wide open. This is the deepest level of rapport.

The *physical body* communicates with gestures and actions. Again, commonality opens the door to deeper levels of rapport. Gestures and body language are so important that they affect us both on the physical level and at the conscious or intellectual level. The way we move our body can actually be far more powerful than the words we choose or the tone in which we deliver them.

In fact, behavioral scientists tell us that a full 55% of what we communicate is conveyed through our bodies. Tonality accounts for 38% and words count for a mere 7%. If you find this hard to believe, think about it. Has anyone ever told you something and for some unknown reason, you just didn't believe them? You couldn't put a finger on what it was, but something in their communication just wasn't right. When that happens with me, it's usually because something in their tone or physical body isn't congruent with what they are saying. Our intuitive factor picks up this message, and we just don't believe or trust the other person.

Master communicators send the same message on all three levels: conscious, unconscious, and physical. Their messages are completely congruent. With your closest partners and friends, you probably don't think much about the fact that you have similar gestures and actions, words, energy, or vibration. These things just happen. You can deepen your rapport with new people by creating these same commonalties in words, tonality, gestures, and actions, but by doing so consciously.

COMMUNICATION IS VIBRATION

I learned a lot about communication from my mother, who is a master at communicating through vibration and emotion.

Whenever something is going on in my life – a difficult time in business, struggling to stay focused, or letting little negative thoughts creep into my mind – the phone rings and Mom is on the other end. I don't have to tell her a thing. She knows! She is extremely sensitive to vibrations. She tunes into them and follows her intuition.

Have you ever found yourself thinking of someone, and then the phone rings and they are on the line? That's the Law of Vibration at work. The other person's thoughts of you are in rapport with your unconscious mind, and you are receiving their vibrations across time and space.

Vibration and emotion are the most profound form of communication, and masters make sure that their words, tone, and actions match the vibration they are sending out.

Your relationships are your future. They will guide and inspire you to your success if you allow and nurture them.

SUMMARY
CHAPTER 5: THE POWER OF PARTNERSHIPS

1. No one can succeed alone.

2. Choose business and personal partners who are the people you want to become, and get on the fast track by having a mentor.

3. Use masterful communication on the conscious, unconscious, and physical levels to establish rapport and build deep relationships.

4. Successful people don't compete. They create.

THE POWER OF GIVING

"We make a living by what we get.
We make a life by what we give."
WINSTON CHURCHILL

THE POWER OF PARTNERSHIPS LEADS NATURALLY into the fifth Power Principle, the Power of Giving.

Great world leaders, high achievers, and extremely successful people have always been the greatest givers. Napoleon Hill said, "I will induce others to serve me because of my willingness to serve others."

Ralph Waldo Emerson said, "One cannot sincerely help another without helping himself."

Jesus said, "Let he who would be the greatest among you be the servant of all."

THE GREATEST GIFT

One of the best ways to appreciate the Power of Giving is to remember how it feels when people have given to you.

In 1995, I moved my business from Atlanta to San Diego. It was an important move, but new staff, office space, furniture, and equipment quadrupled my monthly overhead. I had signed two large consulting contracts that would cover all these expenses, but just as the bills started rolling in, both clients suddenly decided that they couldn't do any training in the coming year and canceled their contracts. At that moment, I had no scheduled speaking or consulting dates on my calendar, minimal cash coming in from prior work, and due dates coming up on all my bills. I was definitely being asked to walk my talk, to exercise my faith, and to practice the principles that I teach.

I walked to the mailbox on a particularly low and difficult morning and, among the bills, found an extra large envelope. "Probably an extra large bill," I thought to myself.

Then I saw that it was from one of my closest friends in St. Louis. Inside I found large crayon drawings of myself and my house from his children. "We're thinking of you, James," was scrawled across each paper in broken crayon letters. My friend had written a wonderfully encouraging letter that included a poem about how "God's delays are not God's denials." He had enclosed a CD with Elton John's "Blessed" on it. As I sat in my living room listening to that song, I began to cry. I let myself receive this gift, which I knew came straight from the heart. I had never received a more precious or timely gift, and I realized that the intent behind it, the feelings of love that clearly came with it, were even more important than the gift.

My friend's gift got me back on track. I realized that I'd been caught up in what I *didn't* want, rather than focusing on my vision and all the wonderful things that had come from my move. He gave without expecting anything in return, and he will be blessed because of that. Let's explore further how this principle works.

CAUSE AND EFFECT: THE BOOMERANG PRINCIPLE

The Law of Cause and Effect says that every effect has a cause, and every cause has an effect. It can also be stated as The Boomerang Principle, which says that what you put out into the universe comes right back into your life. Put out a lot and you get a lot back. Put out a little and you get a little back.

The problem is that many people give a little and expect a lot back. This never works, and so they are always disappointed.

Giving is one of the most powerful principles in the Science of

Success for two reasons:

1. If you give great service and value to others, you will receive great returns.

2. Giving is one of the quickest ways to plant new ideas and new realities of abundance into your unconscious mind. When you give, you tell your unconscious that you have more than enough and that you live in total abundance. You don't have to hoard, guard carefully what you have, be stingy, or hold back in any way. You can always attract to yourself more than you need – at any time, and from an unlimited supply.

THE BOOMERANG IN ACTION

The story of Graebel, a worldwide moving company, from Eric Fellman's *The Power Behind Positive Thinking*, is a great illustration of the Boomerang Principle.

Graebel Companies was growing quickly and finally landed their first million dollar contract! They were going to move a huge company from one city to another. It was the biggest move Graebel had ever done, and CEO David Graebel invested in six new trucks and hired extra crew for packing, loading, and driving. He made massive changes within the company to accommodate this monumental effort. Two days before the move, David got what he called "the worst phone call of my career." The president of the large company told him, "On Monday morning, we're filing for Chapter 11 bankruptcy protection, and we won't be able to honor our contract."

David sat at his desk, stunned. The world seemed to be crashing down around him. Finally, he came up with a plan. News of the canceled contract spread like wild fire in the company, and David called an emergency meeting of the six regional sales managers.

They arrived at headquarters in a cloud of doom.

David opened the meeting by saying, "Isn't this fantastic? What an opportunity we have!" The sales managers looked at each other warily, but David continued undaunted. "Do you realize that just a few years ago, we only had a few trucks operating out of Wausau, Wisconsin, and barely two nickels to rub together at the end of the month? Not so long ago, a million dollars was more than we made in a whole year. Now here we are, having lost a million dollar contract in one day, and we're still in business! In fact, we're doing so well that we can afford to fly you all in to work out what to do about the problem."

They mindstormed the issue, and the team decided to go forward with moving the large company as planned. The president of this company listened in disbelief as David told him, "We're more interested in having you as a long-term client than we are in making one very profitable deal. We're going to move you, just as we planned. We'll submit our bill and get in line with all the other creditors."

The move was a huge success. News of Graebel's efforts got around, and within nine months they had generated nearly a million dollars in new business! They had also been paid 30% of the large company's moving bill.

Graebel gave generously to the large company because he felt it was the right thing to do, and the Boomerang Principle gave back to him from sources other than those to which he had given!

Two years later, the president of the large company called David and said, "A couple years ago, I called you with some pretty bad news. Today I wanted to be the first to call you with some good news. We're announcing next Monday that we're coming out of Chapter 11. Even though we're free of the legal obligations, we're going to work hard over the next year to repay you 100% of the outstanding balance. Your work was the key to getting us back on our feet so quickly."

By giving, Graebel attracted more good than he ever could have imagined.

Giving not only sets the Law of Cause and Effect in motion, it also brings the Law of Attraction into play. This law states that the good you give *must* come back to you. If you give a fortune in value to people, it is absolutely appropriate for you to collect a fortune in return.

Some people are reluctant to charge what they are worth, especially when what they are offering is worth a lot! This attitude is either part of some old, limiting "money is evil" or "I am not worthy" thinking or the result of fear that if they charge what they are worth, no one will be able to afford them. Both of these thoughts are in error. They restrict your ability to receive and others' ability to give.

Think again about George Bernard Shaw's statement that, "It is a sin to be poor." We live in a world that rewards us monetarily for the product or service we provide to people. So in our world, being poor means that you are not *giving* enough value to others. The opposite side of this coin is that we run into problems when we try to charge a fortune for what we do but do not provide people with a fortune worth of value.

Resolve to charge and accept every penny that you are worth and to deliver more than the value for which you charge.

WINNERS ALWAYS PROVIDE TEN TIMES MORE VALUE

Winners always give ten times more value than what they ask in return.

The paper and ink that make up this book may not be worth the amount you paid, but the concepts contained within it are worth a fortune! And when you consistently apply these concepts, they will impact your life forever.

Successful people provide ten times more to their clients, or to other people with whom they interact, than they ask for in monetary compensation. Who wouldn't want to work with or be around someone like that? Regardless of the investment, their clients and associates always feel that what they received is worth far more than whatever they paid. In fact, the clients of true winners often feel that they *underpaid* for what they received.

For this reason alone, your business will be a huge success if you understand and use the Power of Giving. People love to tell their friends about getting a great value, so winners get a lot of referrals and don't have to do as much marketing as others do. When someone gives you tremendous value, don't you feel like telling someone you care about? Wouldn't you send a family member to someone who treated you well, handled your business with excellence and passion, and gave you ten times what they asked in return?

THE HOWARD FACTOR

Howard is a great example of giving ten times more value. I first met him at Wolfgang Puck's world-famous restaurant in San Diego, where he was the manager.

That evening a hurried waiter came around the corner and spilled part of a salad on my shirt. Howard was at my side immediately. He apologized and asked me to send him the dry cleaning bill. He even offered to replace the shirt, if necessary, and picked up our dinner for five!

A few weeks later, I returned to Wolfgang Puck's. Howard recognized me and showed us to a table immediately. He picked up our dinner for two that night, and later in the week I received a check for the dry cleaning and a $25 gift certificate for dinner at Wolfgang Puck's.

Howard invested a lot in keeping me as a customer, far more

than the cost of getting my shirt cleaned, which was what he "owed" me. But what has he gained in return? I keep going to his restaurant, and I refer people there all the time. I've mentioned him in this book, and he gets recognition all over the world as I tell his story in my presentations. That's worth a lot more than some free meals and a dry cleaning bill.

Howard never asked for anything in return for what he gave, but the value he gave came back to *him* multiplied by ten.

GIVING IS NOT TRADING

Giving is offering something to someone for the joy of contributing. Trading is offering something with the expectation of getting something back.

When people do not experience the true joy of giving or the returns that are inevitable when they give, it is often because their "giving" is really trading. They have a hidden agenda of getting something back, preferably in the same amount or better than what they gave. They trade their love, friendship, gifts, or services expecting something in return, usually right away, and usually from exactly the person to whom they "gave." They haven't really given, so they rarely receive in return. This often happens in relationships. What we call "love" can actually be trading if someone is thinking, "I'll give you this if you will give me that in return."

Other people "give" simply because they think it's what is expected of them. Think about the holidays in your family. Do some family members go out and buy gifts just because they think someone else is going to give them one? They don't really want to give; they're just worried about looking bad if they get a gift without giving something in return. This isn't really giving either. To them, it's all about preventing embarrassment or judgment.

True giving comes from the heart. The gift doesn't have to be huge or elaborate. It just has to come from the heart. The return often comes back to you in mysterious, unexpected ways, and often from an entirely different source from the one to which you gave.

Real winners understand the Law of Giving and have faith that it will work. They know that if they give, they will receive, but that's not why they give. They give for the sheer joy of helping others and providing something of value. For the most successful people, giving itself is the reward.

How can you give more to the people in your life? How can you give ten times more value than what you ask in return? Make a list. Be both specific and creative.

THE VACUUM LAW OF PROSPERITY

If you want to bring something new into your life, you must have some space available for it. Nothing can come into your life unless there is room for it. Nature abhors a vacuum. If you make space, something will come to fill it.

You can test this principle easily by going out into your backyard and digging a hole. What happens? It won't be long before the hole begins to fill in. Why? Nature fills the void. When I hear, "Nature abhors a vacuum," I often think of my kitchen counter. I clean it off and it looks great. It's absolutely spotless. But it never stays that way for long. My desk is the same way. I get it all cleared off, and within days the mail begins to stack up. Books and other items get stacked on it. The point is that anything that we leave empty begins to fill.

A wonderful Bible story shows us the difference between wishing for something and being prepared to receive it. When Moses was leading his people out of Egypt, they found themselves wandering and lost, without water and with no rain in sight. The people came to Moses, pleading with him to intercede with God on their behalf. Moses calmly told them to pray for rain. They prayed, but no rain came. They went back to Moses and said, "Our prayers don't work. Where is the rain?"

Moses replied, "Where are the ditches?"

The people were confused, and said, "We don't understand. We need rain."

Moses repeated, "Where are the ditches? If you really believed that God would bring rain, you would have dug ditches!"

To receive all the good that your heart desires, you must believe and be prepared to receive it. And you must create a space for it to fill when it arrives.

This is actually the fun part. Think about how you can create large or small vacuums in your life to house the good that is already on its way to you. There is no better way to send a message of abundance to the universe and to your unconscious than to give away things that no longer serve you or represent who you are. What are you hanging onto that no longer serves you?

VACUUM CLEANING

Cleaning out your closet and giving away what you no longer use is a great way to create space for your good and to enjoy the pleasure of giving at the same time. Every article of clothing you give away makes room for things that *do* serve you and represent who you are now.

How many old suits, shirts, slacks, skirts, blouses, or shoes do you have in your closet that don't serve you anymore? How many are not appropriate for your new mindset or your vision? Yet as you go into the closet and start to pull them out, you may think, "Oh, maybe that'll come back in style." I've certainly done that. The problem is that you are sending a message to your unconscious that if you give it away, you may not be able to replace it. That's a message of scarcity.

Why not send a message of abundance to your unconscious? Say to yourself that if something isn't serving you anymore, you can afford to get rid of it and make room for something better. You have access to an unlimited supply, so you can replace it anytime you want. You know that everything comes from one single source, and you can tap into that source whenever you want.

What can you do with those old clothes? Sell them? Hock them at a garage sale? No, you *give* them away. You don't need money for them. You can replace them anytime you want, pulling from your endless supply.

Go into your closet, find everything you haven't worn in the last year: those old plaid bell-bottoms or platform shoes, perhaps, and anything that doesn't exactly fit you anymore. Take those old clothes and give them away. If they are "ten pounds too light" for you or if you wouldn't be caught dead wearing them, give them away. Give them to someone who will get pleasure and value from them.

One time, I went to my closet and saw a lot of shoes that were like new but that I hadn't worn in a long time. I just gave them away, and it felt great! Before long, I had all new shoes and my closet was filled again. I enjoyed giving them to people who needed and appreciated them more than I did. I had the time of my life, and that's part of the giving process.

Recently the woman who takes care of the plants in my home mentioned that one of her friends had moved into a new place and was looking for furniture. I asked her spontaneously, "Hey, does he need a couch?"

"Yes, as a matter of fact he does," she answered.

"Would he like this one?" I asked, pointing to the one in my den.

"Sure, I bet he would," she answered. "What do you want for it?"

"He can just have it," I said. "If he'll haul it away, it's his."

Giving away that couch created a huge vacuum in my den, and it wasn't two weeks before I had a brand new couch: one I like a lot and enjoy tremendously.

The Vacuum Law of Prosperity applies to more than closets and couches. You can use it to draw good into every area of your life. Test it by doing some of your own vacuum cleaning!

SCARCITY VS. ABUNDANCE

People's attitudes toward giving reflect whether they think about life in terms of abundance or in terms of scarcity. We have seen that all great achievers have been great givers, and that giving is the best way to send a strong message of abundance into the universe.

People who have a mentality of scarcity always feel that they must hold onto things. They feel the need to hoard and save. They often think only of themselves. And not surprisingly, that is what the Law of Attraction brings to them. Like attracts like. Hoarders are afraid of losing what they have, so that's what often happens. Givers, on the other hand, only attract more good. Lao Tzu once said, "To take, you must first give."

Which mentality do you have: scarcity or abundance? An abundance mentality tells you that everything in the universe comes from the same source of supply and that supply is unlimited. You and everyone you know could become multi-millionaires, and there will still be billions of dollars to go around. You and everyone you know can create the life of your dreams, and it won't prevent anyone else from being happy. You can be, do, and have everything you want, and there will still be bountiful goodness and abundance for everyone on Earth. *Nothing can ever truly be lost except opportunity.*

Here are some questions to ask yourself in order to start putting the Power of Giving at your disposal:

- How can you give more in your professional life? Think of ways to make a positive impact on your boss, your peers, your clients, and your customers. What are some specific things you can give these people?

- What specifically will you do, and by when?
- How can you give more in your personal life, to your family, your friends, and yourself?
- What specifically will you do, and by when?
- Finally, make a list of all the reasons that these commitments are vital to your success.

Giving is one of the most powerful things you can do for yourself. Winston Churchill said, "We make a living by what we get. We make a life by what we give."

SUMMARY
CHAPTER 6: THE POWER OF GIVING

1. The Boomerang Principle brings back to you all that you give and more.

2. Winners give ten times the value that they ask in return. They give rather than trade, and they contribute to others from the heart.

3. To make room for your good, create a vacuum by giving away the things that no longer serve you.

4. Adopt an attitude of abundance, and never entertain thoughts of scarcity.

THE POWER OF GRATITUDE

*"When you feel grateful, you become great,
and eventually attract great things."*

PLATO

THE POWER OF GRATITUDE IS THE SIXTH Power Principle in the Science of Success. The great Roman statesman Marcus Tullius Cicero said, "Gratitude is the mother of virtues."

Gratitude is not only the mother of virtues, it is the mother of all life's benefits. It brings love, health, happiness, and prosperity. Wherever you find truly successful individuals, you find gratitude in large quantities. Gratitude sets up a field of attraction more powerful than any other, attraction so strong that it cannot help but bring your vision to you.

The other side of this coin is that lack of gratitude can be extraordinarily disempowering. If we're not careful, we can forget all the goodness that comes into our lives. Concentrating attention on what you *don't* have, rather than on what you *do* have, throws your whole system into a negative vibration and a state of imbalance. According to the Law of Attraction, people who are not grateful tend to attract and manifest the very thing they fear and abhor most: lack, in all its forms. They think about lack, so they manifest lack.

To experience gratitude on a continuing basis, you must understand and believe three truths:

1. Your current situation is great and getting better.

2. Your current life is full of things for which to be grateful.

3. Your current results will continually change, grow, and improve.

Let's look at these one at a time.

YOUR CURRENT SITUATION IS GREAT AND GETTING BETTER

According to the Law of Relativity, our reality is only created by comparison. We can be grateful or ungrateful for whatever our situation is. Some people might feel completely blessed and grateful for a salary of $70,000. Others might feel very dissatisfied with that amount.

Bottom line, we all have many things for which to be grateful. We are alive. Most of us have connections with other people, enough to eat, a place to rest, and clothes on our backs. In order to get into an ungrateful frame of mind, we have to forget all those things and focus on the very limited number of things with which we are *not* satisfied.

For instance, you may not be satisfied with your current income. The only way you can be dissatisfied is to compare it to something else, to judge it against some arbitrary criteria. There is nothing wrong with wanting to improve your income, but it's not really useful to think of that amount of money as either too great or too little. It may not be exactly what you want, but it is probably quite substantial compared to the average annual income of $180 in Bangladesh. When you look at it in that light, your feelings about it may change.

Your current situation is whatever *your past thoughts* and actions have caused it to be. It is neither good nor bad. It just is. It has nothing to do with what your income will be in the future and no real meaning except the meaning that you assign to it. Since you can choose to be either grateful or ungrateful, why not choose a frame of mind that will start drawing more good to you? An attitude of gratitude is one of the most powerful magnets in the universe. Use it to attract more of whatever you want.

As you start being actively grateful for all the good in your life, know that even more good is on its way. When you send out these positive and grateful vibrations, you cannot fail.

YOUR CURRENT LIFE IS FULL OF THINGS FOR WHICH TO BE GRATEFUL

To experience ongoing gratitude, it's important to remember that your life is *full* of things for which to be grateful. Make a practice each day of remembering, and perhaps even listing, all the things for which you are grateful. Know that whatever you don't like is only temporary, merely the result of your past thoughts and actions, and that you are in the process of changing it.

The reason many people lack gratitude is that they negate all the good things they currently have and focus only on the areas they want to improve. Instead, focus on all the riches that you currently have in your life. For example, think about your eyesight. How much would you pay to get it back if it were lost? What would the ability to walk or run be worth to you if it were gone? What price would you pay for a loving and faithful family and friends? What is your health worth? What would you pay to have it back if you were diagnosed with a terminal illness? If you can see, walk, love, and get out of bed each morning, you are rich beyond measure.

To experience gratitude in finances, we need only remember that most of us live in sumptuous wealth compared to most of the rest of the world. To experience gratitude for the process of living, we need only remember our marvelous minds, which can comprehend the Super Laws and begin to create whatever we desire. We can acquire all the books and knowledge we want. We can get all the education we desire, so that we continually expand and grow. We live in a country that treasures free enterprise, and in which we can choose or change our careers at will. We can pursue our passions without interference, and create anything our minds and spirits can dream. These are vast riches.

One of the things I do each morning is to ask myself the question, "What am I grateful for today?" It's a much more empowering question than, "Why do I have to get up so early?" or "Why didn't I get to bed at a decent time last night?" or "Why do I have to go to work today?" I encourage you to ask each morning for thirty days, "What am I grateful for today?" It will help you remember all the things you appreciate in your life. Try it right now. What are you grateful for today? Answer the question as it relates to your health, your abilities, your business, your family, and your friends.

Here are some other questions to consider:

- How does a lack of gratitude set the Law of Attraction in motion to create what you don't want, instead of what you do want?

- How is an attitude of gratitude a powerful magnetic force for greatness in your life?

- How will you remember to be continually grateful?

Remembering who you are and what you have at your disposal helps you experience gratitude for all your glorious gifts.

YOUR CURRENT RESULTS WILL CONTINUALLY CHANGE, GROW, AND IMPROVE

The third important belief in the Power of Gratitude is that your current circumstances are the result of your past thinking and actions. Since your thinking is improving, your results will improve as well. The results you have today do not represent your future!

When you sink into negative thinking and become ungrateful for your current state of affairs, you send your unconscious the message, "I do not believe that my dreams and vision are on the way. What I have is permanent and will not change or improve." This thinking becomes a self-fulfilling prophecy. You end up manifesting your worst fears: lack and limitation. Instead, plant the seeds of gratitude, belief, and faith in the magnificent garden of your mind, and watch those seeds take root.

If you truly have faith and belief in your ability to succeed, you will be grateful in *advance*. And being grateful in advance nurtures your faith and belief. Your unconscious mind begins creating exactly what you ask and expect.

We always manifest our greatest desire through gratitude or our worst fear through lack of gratitude. The law works every time, either for us or against us. Your controlling idea will *always* manifest into physical reality.

FAITH IN ACTION

Gratitude activates the power of faith. You know your good is on the way, so your unconscious sets the universe in motion to fulfill your desire. You can see this dynamic at work every day. When you meet someone who is tremendously grateful for everything he or she has right now, even if circumstances are not currently ideal, what message do you receive? You probably receive a positive vibration and an intuition that this person is confident of getting what he or she wants. Doesn't that inspire you to want to be around the person and even to contribute to their dreams and vision when and if you can? This is what I call "faith in action." The Bible tells us, "Whatsoever you shall ask in faith, believing, you shall receive."

When you are completely grateful, your unconscious receives the message, "I may not like my current results, but I know that they are nothing more than the outcomes of my past thinking. Because they are temporary, I can be completely grateful. I know the good I choose is coming into my life."

When you live in this state of mind and luxuriate in gratitude, you can relax, enjoy, and appreciate your journey in life. Your new thinking is attracting the good you seek and deserve. You can find the beauty in every person, place, thing, and moment. Grateful people are powerful people, and they are a joy to be around.

Conversely, people who are not grateful for their good tend to put out a negative vibration and attract negative results. One of the people in our family never showed gratitude for the gifts she received. At Christmas, she took her presents for granted and rarely showed any appreciation or excitement. It wasn't long before none of the family had much desire to give her gifts. It was more fun to buy things for other family members who were thrilled to receive whatever they were given. Whether you are dealing with a family member or a restaurant server, giving out gratitude brings the good back to you.

Gratitude, more than any other state of mind, keeps us connected to our good. By staying in an attitude of gratitude, we focus on all the good that is already in our lives and, by law, begin to attract more of the same. Gratitude is the ultimate faith.

THE PRINCIPLE OF APPRECIATION

This principle helps you turn the attitude of gratitude into a habit by giving the good in your life attention and appreciation.

The Law of Rhythm tells us that everything in nature and in our lives is either growing or dying. Stated simply, this Super Law says, "Create or disintegrate." Whatever is not growing, is dying. We are always moving in one direction or the other.

We also know that the way to make things grow is to give them energy and attention. You can see this even with your houseplants. When you give them energy and attention, they flourish and grow. Everything in life has a craving to be appreciated, from plants to animals to people. Whatever receives that energy and attention grows.

Appreciation is one of the highest forms of attention. It is a strong and important subset of gratitude. If we do not give attention and appreciation to the good in our lives, it starts to die. When we do give attention and appreciation to our good, it grows. It's just that simple.

Most of us have seen firsthand that appreciation is one of the best ways to strengthen our relationships. When we don't appreciate our spouses, children, family members, business associates, friends, or selves, those relationships begin to die. They respond immediately when we give them appreciation, so we need to pay attention to them.

Who needs the most attention and appreciation in your life? It's the people with whom you spend the most time. It's your children, your family members, your spouse, and your co-workers. Unfortunately, these are often the people we take for granted. A gift once or twice a year isn't enough. It's not the big trips or the big gifts that make people feel appreciated; it's the little things you do every day. True appreciation doesn't have to be anything fancy or grandiose. Small things done consistently, with the right focus, create the strongest impact.

Some of the easiest ways to let others know you appreciate them are also some of the most frequently neglected. A simple "Thank you," fulfilled promises, common courtesy, card, small remembrance, or frequent communication are all ways to build your relationships with others. Eating healthy, exercise, rest, and recreation are important ways to build your relationship with yourself.

Remember, nothing in the universe stands still. Everything is dynamic. If we are not *appreciating* our lives, relationships, and circumstances, they are *depreciating*. Here are some good questions to ask yourself:

- What do you most appreciate about your spouse or significant other? How will you show it more effectively and more often?

- What do you most appreciate in your children? How will you show it more effectively and more often?

- What do you most appreciate in your family? How will you show it more effectively and more often?

- What do you most appreciate in your closest friends? How will you show it more effectively and more often?

- What do you most appreciate about your health? How will you show it more effectively and more often?

- How do you believe that appreciation will attract more of what you want in your life?

- Why are gratitude and appreciation vital parts of achieving your vision?

"LITTLE" APPRECIATIONS

Remember the philosophy that "little things mean everything"? It's true for appreciation as well.

I have always tried to make my clients feel like they are the most important people in the world, and part of that is staying in touch with them in creative ways. It just takes a little time and thought, and it's well worth the effort, for me and for them. Some of the ways I connect with them are through hand-written cards (my favorite), e-mail, thoughtful gifts, and phone calls. The key to appreciation is to be original and sincere. An "all I want is your business" call, disguised with phony sincerity, usually feels like exactly that.

I recently got a call from a client with whom I had not done business in more than three years. Many people would have written this person off long ago, but I stayed in touch. As my own business began to develop into new arenas, I kept him informed. One of my "touching base" phone calls came at a time when he was planning an annual sales event. I mentioned that I was doing a lot of keynote speaking and asked if he was considering hiring an outside speaker. Long story short, I had three opportunities in a six-month period to speak for the company!

Was it a wise investment to keep in touch and let this man know he was appreciated? You bet. All it took was investing a little time, showing genuine appreciation, and remembering that *the little things mean everything*!

THE HOUSE OF LLOYD

Harry Lloyd is another great example of the power of appreciation. Harry owned the hugely successful House of Lloyd company that centered around home parties for Christmas Around the World catalog items. The company was headquartered in Grandview, Missouri, a suburb of Kansas City, and had about 400 employees.

In February of 1997, Harry Lloyd called a plant-wide meeting just before quitting time on a Friday. He told his employees that on the following Monday morning, they were to be at Kansas City International Airport with a suitcase packed for a week. Each of them could bring one guest. Everyone was invited, from housekeepers to top executives. The plant would be closed for the week, and a private security firm was hired so that even the regular security guards could go on the mystery trip. If people couldn't leave town for some reason, they would be paid for a week's vacation plus as much as was being spent on the people who went on the trip.

On Monday morning, 350 people and their guests showed up at the airport and boarded four chartered 737s. Once in the air, the pilots announced that their destination was Acapulco! Most of these people had never been on an airplane, let alone to Mexico!

In Acapulco, they all had ocean-front rooms at a beach hotel. The first night, there was a buffet dinner and entertainment on the beach. Everyone was given $500 spending money, and everything they ate or drank at the hotel that week went on Harry Lloyd's tab. Thursday night, a few people spotted a beautiful cruise ship all lit up out in the bay and said what a thrill it would be to be on board a ship like that.

Friday morning, Harry told everyone he wanted to have dinner with them that night and asked them to meet him on the beach at dusk. When they arrived, they were whisked off by helicopter and small boats to the cruise ship, where they were wined and dined and danced all night! They returned home to Kansas City the next day with memories they would never forget and a deep sense of how much Harry appreciated them.

Harry Lloyd had been told two weeks before the trip that he was dying of cancer, and he had wanted to leave this life knowing that the people who worked for him knew the depth of his gratitude. He gave 700 people the thrill of their lives, and they will never forget him or his moving gesture of appreciation.

SUMMARY
CHAPTER 7: THE POWER OF GRATITUDE

1. Gratitude is a powerful magnetic force to attract the good you desire.

2. To experience gratitude on a continuing basis, you must understand and believe three truths:

   • Your current situation is great and getting better.

   • Your current life is full of things for which to be grateful.

   • Your current results will continually change, grow, and improve.

3. Faith in action is being grateful before your good comes to you.

4. Appreciation makes gratitude a habit and nourishes the goodness in your life.

THE POWER OF
ACCOUNTABILITY

"The price of greatness is responsibility."
WINSTON CHURCHILL

YOU NOW HAVE ALL OF THE SUPER LAWS and six of the Power Principles. This final Power Principle, the Power of Accountability, is the last piece of the puzzle. It sets The Science of Success in motion and opens the combination lock to the life of your dreams.

When I was a kid, I always loved making that last turn in the lock for my bike or school locker. As I turned to that last number, I felt a surge of excitement. The lock *clicked* in a different way, and the lock opened almost by itself! This is exactly where you are with The Science of Success. All you have to do is turn the dial and the lock will open.

The Power of Accountability is about results. My dear friend and mentor Bob Proctor once told me, "Results tell an interesting story... they tell the true story."

The Science of Success produces results, but only if you *use* the principles and consistently put them into action. If you don't use them, if you aren't accountable to yourself for living in alignment with the Super Laws and practicing the Power Principles, then you won't get the results. It's up to you to learn and understand the program, and to practice it in your life. No one can make you do that, and no one can do it for you. You are absolutely in control of your own destiny. It's a matter of choice, not chance.

Being accountable means that you take responsibility for all the results in your life. You don't blame others if things don't work out. You understand that you, and nobody else, have produced the life you live today. This means that you adopt the belief that you literally create everything that happens to you, and that it's all part of a larger plan for your good, even if you aren't completely there yet in your mind and heart.

You might say, "Well, I can't help who my parents were, or how they brought me up." According to the Principle of Accountability, you actually did choose your parents and circumstances on some larger scale, and you chose them for a good reason: either to learn a lesson yourself or to help them grow. This is easy for some people to accept and harder for others to embrace.

Successful people have always understood and practiced the Principle of Accountability. *Only when you are accountable for everything in your life can you be responsible to change or control your life.* If you had nothing to do with bringing your current circumstances into existence, then there is nothing you can do to change them. It is crucial to understand that if anything is going to happen in your life, it is entirely up to you.

This is not a common or popular belief. I interact with individuals and organizations every day, and very few people are willing to step up and be accountable for their lives. Yet, I suggest to you that *until and unless you do just that, you will never create what you truly want.* You can't claim the power to create what you want in the future unless you are willing to be accountable for having created *less* than what you wanted in the past.

I have a close friend who is very successful. He made his millions in real estate in his mid-twenties and has moved on to other passions. He told me recently about a very bad investment he had made. It was so bad that he lost $300,000! As I listened to him, I was struck by the fact that he admitted full accountability for what had happened. Never once did he blame the neighbor who had urged him to make this investment or offer any excuses. He just said, "I learned a lot, and after all, I was the one who made the decision. No one twisted my arm!"

I took my friend to the airport the next afternoon, and he flew off to a business meeting where he was offered a huge opportunity that was much larger than his temporary loss of $300,000.

Being completely accountable for his actions even when things didn't go well was a key ingredient in my friend's success. He used everything as a chance to learn, even when those lessons were painful, and it paid off for him very quickly.

TWO KINDS OF PEOPLE: DREAMERS AND ACHIEVERS

I meet thousands and thousands of people each year through my work. Most of them are in one of two categories: dreamers or achievers.

Dreamers dream big dreams, but they don't always follow through and get results. Achievers dream big dreams and turn them into results. They can put it in the bank – financially, emotionally, and spiritually. They are accountable for their lives. They know that nothing is going to happen unless they make it happen. Achievers take *action*. Massive, immediate, intelligent, consistent action! That is the difference between people who dream and people who achieve.

Last year, I gave a morning presentation in Atlanta and had the afternoon off. It was a beautiful spring day, so I walked down to the Chattahoochee River. The sky was clear, the sun was shining, and the birds were singing. As I crossed a bridge, I noticed movement below me in the water. I looked down and saw three kayakers, so I stopped and watched.

Two of them were running a course through some gates, spinning and swerving in and out. From what my amateur eyes could tell, they were doing a great job. There was a third person on the shore, and it was obvious from the way he carried himself and gave instructions to the other two that he was the pro. I thought their performance was outstanding, but he obviously did not.

He lowered himself into his kayak and pushed off from the shore. What happened next was pure poetry. He began to swerve, cut, and spin his kayak in and out of the gates. The water didn't even ripple. He finished the course without a flaw, came back to the shore, and pulled himself out of his boat.

"That's not fair!" said one of the students.

The instructor slowly set down his oar. He looked her straight in the eye and said, "That's not fair? Do you realize what I've been doing for the past seven years while you and your friends were out partying on Friday nights? I was home studying the masters, listening to audio, watching video, and learning this craft. I went to bed early so I could get up Saturday morning and train. I was down here in the gates, practicing and learning my sport. I've put every penny I could for the past seven years into my equipment and training. And do you know what? I wouldn't trade a minute of it. I absolutely love it. It's my passion! I think that it is absolutely fair!"

That instructor was an achiever, and his students were dreamers. It's not enough just to think about prosperity and success. You have to *do* something about it.

We pay a price for greatness. It takes commitment. It takes personal accountability. It takes passion. If you have these qualities and you are willing to be great, to commit, to be personally accountable, and to nurture your passion for success, then join the 3% Club!

THE 3% CLUB: IT'S ALL ABOUT RESULTS

Members of the 3% Club are the 3% of the world's population who hold themselves to the highest standards. They hold themselves accountable for their results every day, in all areas of their lives.

Make a commitment now to be part of this elite club, and start by making a commitment to reread a chapter of this book every day until it plants itself firmly in the garden of your unconscious mind. You might think this is overkill, but it's not. Not if you have the desire and passion to succeed. Your conditioning has been in your unconscious mind for years and years. If you want to replace it, you must be diligent. Replacing your old mindsets with new, unlimited ones takes some time and energy. Remember, weeds grow on their own, but beautiful flowers take nurturing, attention, and commitment.

Recognition is the first law of learning, and repetition is the second. Repetition brings retention. If you want to retain your new mindset and vision, you must apply yourself. To recondition your unconscious mind, you must fill it with new information over and over again.

Do not read or listen to anything that is contrary to these principles. Don't give those weeds a chance! Make the seven Super Laws and the seven Power Principles part of your moment-to-moment thinking. Focus your thinking like a laser, and be accountable for the information you allow into your mind. If you commit to doing this, you will get results.

Winners do what other people do *not* do. They commit and take action. Turbocharged results are guaranteed if you take action and join the 3% Club.

PUTTING WISDOM TO WORK FOR YOU

The difference between dreaming and acting, between those who do not join the 3% Club and those who do, is similar to the difference between knowledge and wisdom that we explored in Chapter 1.

In today's world, many people believe that success comes from what you know. We often hear that knowledge is power. But you and I understand that this isn't true. Knowledge is not power. Knowledge is nothing more than unorganized information. Wisdom is true power. Wisdom is information that is organized and acted upon in alignment with universal principles and laws.

Knowledge is great, but wisdom gets results. Knowledge is what you know. Wisdom is what you're *doing* with what you know.

NO MORE EXCUSES, NO MORE STORIES

Some people have convinced themselves that results aren't necessary. That sounds strange, doesn't it? We all know that to be successful, results are absolutely necessary.

But think about it. How many people do you know who have a good story about why they don't get results. Often the stories started a very long time ago:

- "I grew up in the wrong neighborhood."
- "I didn't get the breaks that everyone else got."
- "My family wasn't as well off as others."
- "I don't have the right schooling or the right degree."

Sometimes these people seem to have fooled themselves into believing that not getting results is acceptable, as long as they have a good story to justify their lack of success. The equation these people seem to use is this: *NO RESULTS + STORIES = RESULTS*. This is absolutely not true, and it is a tremendously disempowering attitude! Some stories sound like great excuses, but they guarantee failure. To the extent that people make excuses for their lack of success, they forfeit the power to *create* success.

Many of the stories we tell are absolutely true. The facts are accurate. And it's also true that people and circumstances outside ourselves may influence us. *But they do not determine our success.* They do not have the power to keep us from our good, unless we let them. Abraham Lincoln, Martin Luther King, and Mahatma Gandhi did not let their very humble beginnings keep them from their dreams. To the extent that we continue to focus on our stories instead of our results, we keep ourselves from changing or achieving anything.

Look at this principle in terms of your own life. Think of an area of life in which you are currently succeeding. It might be in your relationship, your finances, or your tennis game. You might be in great physical shape or be an outstanding parent. Now, to get a closer look at the nature of stories and how irrelevant they are, make up a story about why you are not succeeding in that area. You can probably come up with several good stories about why you might not succeed in that area, an area in which you clearly *are* succeeding. Excuses are always available for those who choose reasons over results.

Winners don't tell stories. Winners push past their stories to get results. Even when adversity comes their way, they don't permit themselves to dwell on excuses.

My friend who lost the $300,000 never once told stories, made excuses, or played the victim. He even told me, "That money I lost is in the safest bank I know of, the 'universal bank.' I know I can and will get it back whenever I need it." This is a great example of how successful people operate and the attitude of accountability that guarantees their success.

Resolve right now to stop using your good stories as excuses. By focusing on your stories, you only create more of the same. Thinking about lack and limitation only creates more lack and limitation. Focus only on your vision and your unlimited potential. The only way to build results is to concentrate consistently on what you choose, to the exclusion of everything else.

Most people are roaring down the highway of life, sitting in the back of the bus with somebody else driving. I'm going to ask you to drive your own bus. This is critical to guarantee that the Science of Success works for you.

People who don't become accountable for their own lives are like ping-pong balls in the surf. They get knocked back and forth by every wave that comes along. They are not in charge of their own destinies.

You and I must choose. We must decide whether or not to become accountable for every single thing that we have in our lives. When we are accountable for the bad as well as for the good, then we can change our circumstances. We can say, "What can I do differently? How can I respond differently?"

So get in the driver's seat. Resolve right now to create your heart's desire.

THE THREE Rs OF ACCOUNTABILITY

The three Rs of accountability are recognition, responsibility, and realizing. Let's look at them one at a time:

- *Recognition:* Your first step is to recognize exactly where you are in relation to your vision. Take an honest look at your current results in five key areas: financial, relational, intellectual, physical, and spiritual. You may want to take a piece of paper and make an accurate assessment of where you are in each of these areas, relative to where you see yourself in your vision.

- *Responsibility:* Being fully responsible for your results is the key to freedom. Take a moment to think about, and perhaps jot down on a piece of paper, exactly why you, and only you, are fully responsible for your past and future results. Call to mind all the great stories you have used as excuses and why these stories have limited you in the past.

- *Realizing:* Realize that you can change and create anything you want. You might want to take some notes on why this is true. Then, write down the new results that you want. This is essentially your vision. What are you looking for in the five key areas: financial, relational, intellectual, physical, and spiritual?

Next, as always, decide what actions you can take in each of these areas. Always take some kind of action within 24 hours of setting a goal. Determine a date by which you can take those actions, and make the commitment to do so.

1. Being accountable means that you take responsibility for all the results in your life.

2. Success comes from being fully accountable and taking action to create the results you want.

3. Let go of excuses and good stories for not succeeding, and adopt the three Rs of accountability: recognition, responsibility, and realizing.

4. Always take some kind of action within 24 hours of setting a goal.

YOUR AWESOME POWER: PUTTING IT
ALL TOGETHER

"There are only two ways to live your life.
One is as if everything is a miracle,
and the other is as if nothing is."
ALBERT EINSTEIN

YOU NOW KNOW EVERYTHING YOU NEED TO KNOW about the Power of Seven: the seven Super Laws and the seven Power Principles. You have all the tools to make your dreams come true and to live the life you want. At this point, people often say to me, "James, I understand the Super Laws and the Power Principles. But what does it look, feel, and sound like to live them on a daily basis?"

In this chapter, I want to review how it looks and feels to actually live these principles and share some realizations I've had over the past few years about the awesome power of people, and give you a few specific suggestions for living the Science of Success.

LIVING THE LAWS

I want to begin by sharing a classic Science of Success story. Barbara Walters interviewed the "star" of this story, and I was struck by how clearly and precisely he had used the Science of Success principles to achieve his dreams.

Barbara began by asking this person if he had always known that he was going to be famous. He said that his passion had always been to be a great actor and entertainer. He had believed in this dream ever since he was a small child, and he had been blessed with close family and friends who also believed that he would be famous and successful someday.

Barbara asked him how he had managed to keep his passion alive when things got tough. This man's childhood had been very difficult. His family had been living the American dream until his father was laid off work. Times got so hard that they started living in the family van, driving from place to place to find work so that they could stay together as a family. They had lost everything except one another. Through those difficult years, this man kept his passion alive by keeping his vision clear.

When he was old enough to be out on his own, he moved to Los Angeles to pursue his dream. To make it real in his mind, he wrote himself a check for $10 million and made a note in the memo corner of the check that said, "For acting services rendered." He put the check in his wallet and kept it there always.

As often as he could, he would go up to Mulholland Drive, overlooking all of Hollywood, and stand gazing out at the city lights. He would take out the check for $10 million and then look out at the lights of the city until he felt as if the money were really his and that everyone in the city knew his name and loved his movies. When he felt the power that came with that belief, he drove back down the hill knowing that he already had his dream.

The night he appeared on Barbara Walters' show, he had just signed a $10 million deal for his next movie. He still had the original check in his wallet when he was actually paid the $10 million real dollars "for acting services rendered."

The actor's name is Jim Carrey, the star of *Ace Ventura, The Mask, Liar Liar,* and *The Truman Show.*

After reading this book, you know that the first check he wrote was as real as the second one he received. It was just a matter of time before the second one arrived. Jim Carrey believed that, and he surrounded himself with people who also believed it. He was grateful for everything he had, even when he didn't have a lot. He applied all of the Super Laws and Power Principles, and the Power of Seven worked for him automatically.

Life is meant to be fun. Jim Carrey knows how to make life fun for himself and other people, both in his work and in his approach to success.

START THE DAY WITH VISIONS

People with whom I work often ask me how I apply The Science of Success in my own life. I answer them by describing my day. It's probably not much different from yours in a lot of ways.

I get up at about 5:00 AM. When the alarm goes off and I reach to turn it off, the first thing I see is my vision card. I've written down my vision on a small card, and I keep it propped up on my nightstand. I close my eyes, get a picture of my vision, and spend a few moments *becoming* that vision, imagining myself within it, already living that life.

Then as I'm getting up, I usually ask myself, "What am I grateful for today?" This is a powerful question. I might be grateful that my bedroom has a spectacular view of the ocean. The colors of the water are always different, but they are always beautiful, and I never get tired of that sight. I find that just asking the question about gratitude reconnects me with how fortunate I am for my work, my friends and family, and my ability to share my life with people.

I have a prayer or affirmation that I repeat to myself in the morning and throughout the day: "I am one with God. God's infinite wealth, love, and wisdom flow in and through me in avalanches of abundance, because I am one with God and God is everything." You might want to make up your own personal statement, or you are welcome to use this one.

Next, I work out. It doesn't matter whether or not you go to a gym. It only matters that as you go through your day, you are doing things you love and that are moving you toward your vision. I pick a great book that will plant positive seeds in my mind and read it while I'm on the exercise bike. I use my vision card as a bookmark, and every once in awhile I'll stop and read my vision, always holding in my mind the picture of what it feels like to be living that life. As I get dressed, I stand in front of my bedroom mirror. I look myself straight in the eye and read my goals, believing that I already have them.

I usually begin working by about 7:30 AM or 8:00 AM. The office and I work long hours, have lots of fun, and help each other out. Some of my greatest relationships and partnerships are built around people who work with us. I never feel as if I *have to* work. It's always a joy, because we practice what we preach.

We have our purpose statement hanging in a picture frame. It's nothing fancy, but we hang it in different spots in the office so we don't take it for granted.

I want you to know that we do not just sit around all day in a dream state, thinking of our visions with our eyes glazed over! We do the same kinds of things that you probably do. We make phone calls, set up meetings, and have appointments. But all the while, we hold our vision in mind. The purpose statement and dream board are just tools to help plant ideas into the unconscious, so that we set in motion the Laws of Attraction and Vibration. We focus on what we're doing *right now*, but we stay connected with our dreams and make sure that every action we take is moving us toward them.

DREAM BOARDS

Dream boards are a great way to use the picturing power of the mind to create your goals and dreams. They let you speak to your unconscious in its own language. I fill my dream board with pictures of everything I want to be, do, and have. The pictures come from magazines, postcards, photographs, and anything else I see that resonates with my vision.

I have all kinds of things on my dream board. One is a picture of two people looking out over the Grand Canyon. I went on a float trip there a couple of years ago, and I want to go back. I had a picture of this book on my board, too, and now you are holding it in your hands. I have a couple pictures of cars and a Harley-Davidson Fat Boy. I have them in my mind right now, and it's just a matter of time before they are sitting in my garage. I also have pictures of my favorite vacation spots and a canceled check from one of my big clients for a very substantial amount. I have a replica of a $100,000 bill from the U.S. Mint and pictures of myself standing on special spots overlooking different cities where I want to build my dream homes.

Think about what you would put on your dream board. Make your pictures colorful and vivid. Make them emotional! The more vividly they live in your mind, the more quickly they materialize.

KEEPING ON TRACK WITH YOUR VISION

People often ask me, "How do you focus on your dreams and at the same time focus on what is before you *right now*?"

I think of it this way. Suppose you were going to drive from San Diego to Atlanta. You wouldn't just look at a map of Atlanta to do that. You'd probably look at a map of the whole route between San Diego and Atlanta. But while you were actually driving, you would keep your eyes on the road just ahead of you. You'd constantly check the road signs to make sure you were going the most efficient way, but your vision would be focused on the road you were actually traveling at the time. You would understand the whole route, but your attention would be on where you were right now.

You hold your vision strongly in your mind, but give 100% attention to whatever you're doing right now, to the things that move you in the direction of your vision. It's a little like patting your head and rubbing your stomach, but it gets easy with practice.

When you begin to see your vision clearly, you may be tempted to do something radical, like leave your job. I don't recommend that you do that. Take it slowly, and don't make any overly quick or dramatic moves. In fact, if something feels like you're jumping off a bridge, take another look at whether you're jumping at an opportunity or whether you actually are jumping off a bridge! Trust your gut feeling, your intuition. I'm not suggesting that you'll never experience fear or take a leap of faith, but you should move at whatever pace feels right for you.

As you give everything you have to today's tasks, you will start to grow. If you want a sure-fire way to change jobs or careers for the better, do the very best you can at the job you have right now. The greatest way to move to a new position in life is to outgrow your current position. Live and give in constant gratitude, and hold your vision clearly in your mind and in your heart. Your focus and clarity will pull your dream to you faster than quitting in anger or frustration.

LETTING THE LAWS WORK

It's tempting sometimes to "push" the Super Laws, to try "forcing" them to work. But it's a lot easier and more fun just to let them do their thing. I have learned that force negates.

In our office, we find that the Super Laws work more quickly and dramatically when we just concentrate on what we're doing and get excited about it. We were sitting around talking recently about various things we wanted to do, and the fact that we needed some additional funds to do them. That very afternoon, FedEx brought us an unexpected check from a client. They just wanted to make sure that they had secured our services, so they sent us an advance deposit. Once you get excited, you move into "the zone" in which the Super Laws accelerate and your goodness comes in *avalanches*.

When my brother first started using the Super Laws, he was

very excited about the Science of Success. One part of his vision was to build a real estate empire. He needed someone to do odd jobs around his rental properties, but he had just moved to a new city and didn't know anyone.

One day he had a flat tire on his way home from work. A bad thing, right? Not at all. The guy who pulled over to help him seemed friendly. They started talking and building rapport. It turned out that this guy's business was doing odd jobs at rental properties. That was exactly what my brother needed! They started working together, and they have a friendly and supportive relationship as well as a strong professional bond.

THE VISION MEDITATION

I've said that the first thing I do each morning is picture my vision in my mind. I do this right before going to sleep as well, and most days I take some time right after lunch to do a little exercise or meditation on my vision.

I'll walk you through the journey I take so that you can duplicate it using your own vision. You may even want to make a CD based on your vision and play it during this quiet time. I take about a half hour, turn off the phones, and sit comfortably in a reclining chair. I get my body and conscious mind very quiet, and then I bring my vision into my mind.

Here's how I would lead someone through the exercise:

Just for a moment, sit quietly with your eyes closed. Quiet your body and your mind. Start at your feet and work all the way up your body, relaxing every muscle. Give your unconscious mind the command. "My feet are totally relaxed. My calves are totally relaxed." Work your way up through the whole body.

Imagine now that you are just waking up. As you open your

eyes, you see that you are in your home with your favorite surroundings outside your bedroom window. It's a crisp, clear morning. You feel the feelings of success and achievement, and you know that you are making a contribution to people's lives with what you do. You feel it, and your body reacts to the power of that feeling.

As you get up, you appreciate all the beautiful furnishings that you see in your home. You are grateful for all the wonderful people and things in your life. You drive through the breathtaking scenery to work and are greeted by people who know you and love you. You check your calendar and are delighted to be meeting with those people today. Your first appointment may be with someone you are mentoring. You feel great that you've taken time to share your wisdom with that person. You see him or her in your mind's eye, smiling with joy. Perhaps your next appointment is with your best client and the next with your own mentor. Your mentor listens well, and you feel yourself lifted to an even higher level.

You stop to buy some fresh flowers before you start home and enjoy the company of loved ones for dinner and a relaxing evening. Before retiring, you relive your vision in your mind and fall into a peaceful, refreshing sleep.

You will want to make this imaging more detailed, and design it more specifically to your own vision. Make it into a moving picture. Have people talk to you. Hear the music, smell the smells, feel the textures. Make your visualization as intense and sensual as possible. See the movie through your eyes, as part of it, not as an observer. Remember, the unconscious mind can't distinguish between something vividly imagined and something that has actually taken place on the physical plane.

I usually end my day by lying down in bed and asking myself a series of questions. What did I do today that contributed to my vision? How did I live my vision? How did I build relationships and partnerships? What did I do that contributed to my relationships and partnerships? How did I give today? Did I give ten times more value than I asked in return? And finally, what am I grateful for? It's a good first question in the morning and a great last question at night.

Then I run through my vision. I get the picture clearly in my mind. I add emotions and sense experiences, and then I hold that picture in my mind as I drift off to sleep.

CHALLENGES MAKE US STRONGER

Many people start practicing the Science of Success but get discouraged the minute they come up against an obstacle. It's important to remember that we will always have challenges, and that we find our greatest strengths when we really commit to a certain course of action and stick with it. Challenges are our greatest teachers. We discover new courage in overcoming them and learning the lessons that they offer us.

As you start to see the Super Laws at work in your life and little changes start to happen, some of your family, friends, and colleagues may not be as happy as you are. They may not understand what you are doing and may even think you are a little crazy. Some of those old relationships may change, and some of the people may even leave. I tell you this so that you will be prepared if it happens to you. It's one of the most common challenges people face when they start to succeed in life.

Know that you are sailing out to sea. Ships were never meant to stay anchored at the dock, and you are doing the right thing. But some people want you to stay back on shore with them. If you keep sailing farther out into the ocean, you may not be as close with them as you once were. That doesn't mean you no longer love them or that you no longer have relationships with them. It just means that your relationship may no longer be as intimate as it once was. You are operating in a different vibration. You are changing and growing, and that's the way it should be. You outgrew some of the toys you enjoyed when you were a child, and this maturing and outgrowing process continues throughout your life. If you focus on the loss, you stop growing. If you focus on the joy of growth, your life keeps expanding.

Another challenge we all face is having the funds to do what we want to do in both our personal and professional lives. I have very aggressive goals, and my company has very aggressive goals. Sometimes that's kind of frightening. My accountant's skill set is just the opposite from mine, but we are both committed to a strong mutual vision. From time to time, he has to tell me that we don't have the funds to finance my grand plans. I want to expand and grow, and he wants to make sure we can pay for it.

We've learned to ask ourselves this question: If money were no object, would this be a good business decision? If the answer is "yes," then we go ahead and do it. We exercise our faith and belief, and trust our intuition. Here's an example. A few years ago, we needed some new training materials that would cost several thousand dollars. At the time, we didn't have the cash available to get it done. But we knew it was a good decision, so we went ahead and got them printed. The very next week, a client called and wanted us to conduct an executive training course immediately! The amazing thing was that the materials they wanted to use in the course were exactly the ones we had just started printing. This contract paid for the cost of printing the materials and much more.

Not only that, but the printing job was going to take about three weeks. If we hadn't already begun the process, we could never have fulfilled our client's need and might have lost the contract. That was the Super Laws in action, and it was thrilling.

I ask myself much the same question in my personal life. "If money were no object, is this decision in alignment with my vision?" Once again, if the answer is "yes," then I go ahead. It's amazing how that decision immediately sets the laws in motion and works to your advantage.

WHAT ABOUT DOUBTS AND NEGATIVE THOUGHTS?

People often ask me what to do about negative thoughts or thoughts that they are unworthy or unable.

I have those thoughts too. We all do. Sometimes they just creep into our minds. The difference now is that I don't let myself dwell on them. I've learned to ask myself when something seems really bad, "Well, what's great about it?" That's the Law of Polarity. If something contains negativity, it also contains just that much positive energy. But sometimes when I ask myself that question, my first answer is, "Nothing!"

So I ask myself another question: "What's great about it if I *really wanted* it to be great?" Almost always, something pops up. In fact, if you check back over your life, you may find that many things that seemed just terrible at the time turned out to be some of the best things that ever happened to you. I know that's true for me. I learned a lot from those events. And sometimes they steered me away from situations that would have actually limited me.

Every failure brings with it the seeds of success. When you get involved in negativity, use the Law of Polarity to turn it around to experience the opposite.

PUTTING YOURSELF ON THE LINE

Living the Science of Success takes courage, because you have to trust the Super Laws before you actually see the results. That's how you attract their power!

In 1995, I was living in Atlanta. I'd left a great upper-management position with a Fortune 500 company and had been on my own for about four years. My business was doing great and most of it was coming to me by referral, or the Law of Attraction. I had a beautiful home with a low mortgage in an upscale neighborhood. Things were going very, very well in Atlanta, but energy is always in a process of changing and transmuting. The Law of Rhythm tells us that if you're not moving forward, you're moving backward. I had hit a plateau, and so I had to make a decision. I had to make a change. I couldn't sit still. My vision spoke to me more loudly than the comfort of my circumstances. I decided to take my career to the next level.

I started to think about what I really wanted to do and how large my vision was, and I knew that Atlanta was not where I needed to be in order to make that happen. About that same time, I went to San Diego on business and my intuition told me that San Diego was where I needed to be! It was a feeling that called me to action. I signed a contract on a home in La Jolla and then went home and put my house on the market. I sold it and moved in six weeks time. I set everything in motion, and the universe handled the details.

I had some trepidation, because I was leaving a great business and wonderful friends. I quadrupled my monthly overhead by moving to La Jolla, and I didn't know anyone there. My faith was tested greatly. I had moved to La Jolla in August of 1995. In December of that year, as I've said, all my clients unexpectedly canceled their contracts. I had brought on new staff and acquired new office space. I'd purchased a lot of new equipment, and made a huge cash outlay.

In February of 1996, I sat in my living room looking around at all the beautiful things I'd bought for the new home, and I just wanted to have the money back! I couldn't make payroll, and I couldn't pay my bills. I even began to doubt my vision.

But here's what I did. I got hold of my thought processes. I realized that you can have a disempowering thought as long as you don't get emotionally involved with it. It won't do much harm if you don't dwell on it and continue to plant it in your unconscious. I learned to cancel my thoughts of scarcity very quickly.

I looked around and came to a defining moment, a moment of truth. I realized that if all my material possessions went away, I would still do exactly what I was doing! My vision truly was still the same, and my passion was still the same. I realized that I couldn't force things to happen, because *force negates*. It's like trying not to think of the pink elephant. That's all you can hold in your mind. If you are trying to force something *not to be*, then you are feeding it energy. I had to relax, trust, and have faith.

That's easy to say when things are going well, but the law operates all the time, when things are going well and when they aren't. It isn't always easy to have faith when things are not going well. I had to make an effort to think in ways that didn't feel comfortable at the time, but those thoughts produced the results I wanted.

I consciously let go of the fear and took hold of my vision. I reclaimed the power of my dreams. I went to the ocean and meditated. I soaked up the beauty of God and nature. I thought about all the things for which I was grateful. It wasn't long before the seeds I planted that afternoon began to attract new clients and new business. I lived, I learned, I laughed, and I let the laws work.

No one has ever experienced greatness without challenging times, and these are the defining moments when we have the opportunity to strengthen our faith, our vision, and our purpose. Remember that those difficult times are the result of your past thoughts and actions. Go forward in faith! Look for the lesson and the blessing. I never would have made the changes I needed to make if I hadn't come to that place where all my assumptions were questioned and reaffirmed. *Challenges come so that we can think about where we are, adjust if we need to do so, and hold to the truth.*

"I am" are the two most powerful words in the English language. Whatever you place after the words "I am" become part of your identity. They get planted deeply into your unconscious mind. My daily prayer, which I shared with you earlier, begins, "*I am* one with God." And the rest is a reflection of that: "God's infinite love, wealth, and wisdom flow in and through me in avalanches of abundance because I am one with God and God is everything." Just like you.

Every year, I take the week between Christmas and New Year's off and go away somewhere that is peaceful and relaxing to reflect on the past year. I set my goals and realign with my vision for the coming year. A few years ago, I went to Sedona, Arizona, and found a rock way up in Boynton Canyon, which the Hopi Indians believed to be sacred ground. It was breathtaking! Very few people go there, because you have to hike all morning to reach it.

I stood on that rock and said my "I am" statements from it. I spoke all the goals and visions that I had just set out from what I now call the "I am" rock. Calling them out into that sacred canyon was incredible.

THE MIGHT OF MENTORING

You've probably heard that we teach what we need to learn. I am fortunate in that my life's mission is the same as my job: to be a teacher. Every day, I get to replant these thoughts into my unconscious mind. You may not be a teacher by profession, but all of us can be mentors. It is one of the greatest contributions we can make to others, and one of the best things we can do for ourselves.

If you want to reinforce your beliefs, vision, and skills, become a teacher to those around you. Find someone who is extremely interested in what you know, and share it with them. Tell them what it means to you. Tell them your story. Tell them what you've learned and how the laws and principles apply to what you're doing. Help them learn. It doesn't matter if you don't think you're ready. You are ready.

We often think of mentoring young people, but you can mentor your contemporaries, your peers, and even people who are older than you. You may have more expertise or experience at something they want to learn. Be generous with your gifts, your skills, and your information.

You will benefit as much or more than they do.

THE POWER OF SEVEN: THE POWER OF YOU

Congratulations! You have just invested more than 97% of the people in the world in the best commodity you could possibly choose: YOURSELF! The rewards you reap will be rich.

I know that, because I have applied these principles in my own life, and they work. For the longest time, I did so at an unconscious level. I wasn't really sure why I was succeeding. Once I learned how to apply the seven Super Laws and seven Power Principles consciously, I could *choose* to succeed. And I could succeed *every time*!

I want to offer you a few parting thoughts by way of reviewing what we have learned. First, remember that the good you are seeking is also seeking you. That is the Law of Vibration and Attraction. Your clarity sets in motion a magnetic force and attracts your vision to you. This is the *Power of Understanding*.

Be constantly aware of your mindset, and be ready to shift it through the *Power of Mindsets*. Imagine and program new, empowering, bigger, and better mindsets as you go forward. Pour in the powerful, clear water of new thought. Use your *Power of Vision* to create clear, vivid pictures of what you want in life.

Nurture relationships through the *Power of Partnerships*. Find mentors and interact with them on a regular basis. Build deep relationships with people you aspire to become, people you admire, and people who will stretch you, believe in you, and help you grow.

Remember that winners don't compete; they create. You truly have no competition.

That will allow you to capitalize on the *Power of Giving*. Winners always give ten times more value than what they ask in return. Remember the Boomerang Principle. Whatever you put out will come right back to you. Create vacuums in your life that will attract the good you seek. Let the *Power of Gratitude* work for you. What are you grateful for today? You will attract more of whatever you appreciate. And finally, understand the *Power of Accountability*. Choose to take responsibility for your own life, your actions, and your results. Drive your own bus. You always have a choice. Give up your good stories forever, and concentrate on getting results.

You are now ready to achieve things that you never imagined possible. You have the power to create anything and everything you want, and you can begin to attract goodness into your life starting *now*. Capture your God-given, unlimited potential and follow your passion.

Thank you for allowing me to share my life, my belief, and my faith with you. My greatest vision is of a world in which people remember who they truly are and that it is their birthright to have whatever they want in life. As each of us grows and moves to a higher personal peak, we advance the entire planet. We all come from the same source and have access to the same power. The greatest contribution you and I can make to the world is to become all that we were born to be. I will be excited to hear of your successes.

Harness your awesome power and make your life a masterpiece!

BIBLIOGRAPHY

Anderson, U.S. *The Magic In Your Mind*. New York: Wilshire Book Company, 1961.

Behrend, Genevieve. *Your Invisible Power*. Montana: Kessinger Publishing, 1927.

Bohm, David. *Wholeness and Implicate Order*. New York: Routledge, 1995.

Capra, Fritjof. *The Tao of Physics*. Boston: Shambhala Publications, 1991.

Castaneda, Carlos. *Journey to Ixtlan*. New York: Washington Square Press, 1972.
A Separate Reality. New York: Washington Square Press, 1971.
The Teachings of Don Juan. New York: Washington Square Press, 1990.
The Art of Dreaming. New York: HarperCollins Publishers, Inc., 1994.

Chopra, Deepak MD. *Quantum Healing*. New York: Bantam Books, 1989.
Unconditional Life. New York: Bantam Books, 1991.
Ageless Body, Timeless Mind. New York; Harmony Books, 1993.

Dyer, Wayne. *Manifest Your Destiny*. New York: HarperCollins

Publishers, 1997.

Frankl, Viktor. *Man's Search for Meaning*. New York: Simon & Schuster, 1984.

Fritz, Robert. *The Path of Least Resistance*. New York: Fawcett Columbine, 1989.
Creating. New York: Fawcett Columbine, 1991.

Goswami, Amit. *The Self-Aware Universe*. New York: Penguin Putnam, Inc., 1993.

Grof, Stanislov, MD. *The Holotropic Mind*. New York: HarperCollins Publishers, 1993.
The Stormy Search For The Self. California: Tarcher/Perigee, 1990.

Hill, Napoleon. *Think and Grow Rich*. New York: Fawcett Crest, 1960.

Holliwell, Raymond. *Working With The Law*. Arizona: Church and School of Christian Philosophy, 1992.

Maltz, Maxwell, MD. *Psycho-Cybernetics*. New York: Pocket Books, 1960.

Mandino, Og. *The Greatest Salesman in the World*. New York: Bantam Books, 1968.

Millman, Dan. *The Way of the Peaceful Warrior*. California: H.J. Kramer, Inc., 1984.

Murphey, Joseph. *The Power of Your Subconscious Mind*. New Jersey: Prentice-Hall, Inc., 1963.

Pirsig, Robert M. *Zen and the Art of Motorcycle Maintenance*. New York: Bantam Books, 1981.

Price, John Randolph. *The Super Beings*. Texas: the Quartus Foundation for Spiritual Research, 1981.

Proctor, Bob. *Born Rich*. Missouri: Praxis International Group, LLC, 1996.

Russell, Robert. *You Too Can Be Prosperous*. California: DeVorss & Company, 1950.

Seligman, Martin. *Learned Optimism*. New York: Pocket Books, 1990.

Sheldrake, Rupert. *The New Science of Life*. Vermont: Park Street Press, 1995.

Talbot, Michael. *The Holographic Universe*. New York: HarperCollins Publishers, 1991.

Troward, Thomas. *The Law and the Word*. California: DeVorss & Company, 1917.
The Creative Process in the Individual. California: DeVorss & Company, 1915.
Bible Mystery Bible Meaning. California: DeVorss & Company, 1913.
The Hidden Power. California: DeVorss & Company, 1921.

Walters, J. Donald. *Money Magnetism*. California: Crystal Clarity Publishers, 1992.

Wattles, Wallace D. *The Science of Getting Rich*. Florida: Top Of The Mountain Publishing, 1993.
The Science of Becoming Excellent. Florida: Top Of The Mountain Publishing, 1993.
The Science of Well Being. Florida: Top Of The Mountain Publishing, 1993.

Wheatley, Margaret. *Leadership and The New Science*. California: Berret-Koehler Publishers, Inc., 1994.

ABOUT
JAMES ARTHUR RAY

AS A SELF-MADE MILLIONAIRE AND BUSI-NESS OWNER, James is one of few spiritual teachers who has achieved top honors in the business world and has thrived as an entrepreneur for over 15 years. His background in behavioral sciences and entrepreneurship, coupled with his avid spiritual quest, gives him a unique and powerful ability to address life issues from an integrated and comprehensive level.

Recently recognized in the *San Diego Business Journal* as one of the fastest-growing entrepreneurial businesses in the area, James Ray International is a multi-million dollar business specializing in teaching individuals how to create wealth in all areas of their life: financial, relational, intellectual, physical, and spiritual.

Prior to his entrepreneurial success, James had a flourishing corporate career, during which he spent over five years as one of AT&T's top sales managers, four years as a personal and business growth expert with AT&T School of Business, and four years working with best-selling author Stephen Covey.

James has studied and been exposed to a wide diversity of teachings and teachers: from traditional college and the business schools of AT&T to the ancient cultures of Peru and Egypt and the jungles of the Amazon. As a result, he has the unique ability to blend the mystical and practical into a usable and easy-to-access formula.

Because of his comprehensive background, James considers himself a "practical mystic." His Journey of Power curriculum is the fusion of wealth-building principles and success strategies, as well as the teachings of all great spiritual traditions, mystery schools, and esoteric studies that James has experienced and assimilated over the last twenty-five years.

When he is not on retreat learning from his spiritual mentors, James conducts more than 150 days of public appearances and seminars each year. As a coach and teacher, James has helped hundreds of individuals and organizations create harmony and wealth in all areas of their business and life.

FOR MORE INFORMATION ON PRODUCTS AND
EVENTS BY JAMES RAY, VISIT WWW.JAMESRAY.COM

A MESSAGE FROM
JAMES ARTHUR RAY

"Aren't you sick of self-improvement programs that promise the moon but fail to deliver any real change in your life?"

JAMES ARTHUR RAY

DEAR FRIEND:

I am, too!

My name is James Arthur Ray, and if you nod your head "yes" to at least some of the following...

...YOU'RE GOING TO LOVE WHAT I'M ABOUT TO REVEAL TO YOU.

- You simply (and deeply) want to make more money and become more successful...

- You want to double, triple, even multiply by ten the size of your business...

- You've already achieved at least a modest level of success and want to use that as a springboard to greater things...

- You know you could do a lot better in life with just a little help...

- You realize that simply working harder can only get you so far, and you want more...

- You know (or at least suspect) that money alone can't buy true happiness...

- You've already made a ton of money but haven't been able to enjoy it like you always thought you would...

- You suspect there's got to be something more to life…
- Your personal relationships can have a huge impact on your overall satisfaction with life…

HAVE YOU EVER THOUGHT ABOUT SUCCESS?

I mean *really* thought about it? Grabbed hold of it with both hands and rolled it over and over and examined it from every angle?

Have you taken it apart and put it back together to see what makes it tick?

Once you did all that, you'd have a pretty good idea of exactly what success is, and how to create it, wouldn't you? Well, that's exactly what I've been doing for the last 25 years and it's been quite a remarkable experience… *and somewhat of a shocking eye-opener!*

IN A MOMENT, I'LL LET YOU IN ON THE MOST AMAZING (AND IMPORTANT) THINGS YOU'LL EVER LEARN ABOUT BECOMING OUTRAGEOUSLY SUCCESSFUL.

Am I qualified to talk to you about success?

Absolutely. You see, 25 years ago I discovered something that had a profound effect on my life (and it's sure to have the same effect on yours, too). I've noticed that virtually all of the most successful people I ever met had several specific traits and beliefs in common with each other.

BIG DEAL, YOU SAY? WELL, IT IS A BIG DEAL.

In fact, this observation is, I believe, the key to the kingdom—the secret that allows nearly anyone to become outrageously successful. Think about it. The best way to become great at anything is to seek out the best people in the field and learn what it is they do that makes them so great—and emulate it.

I'm not saying that a five-foot-six, no-talent, uncoordinated klutz could learn how to be a great basketball player by watching (and trying to emulate) Shaquille O'Neal. Becoming a basketball star requires certain physical and athletic talents that you simply need to be born with.

But I *am* talking about mastering the mental, emotional, and spiritual aspects of becoming successful—*and most people can (and, with my training, do) learn them.*

The more I studied extremely successful people, the more I discovered how alike they are—and how they're different from everyone else.

And as I began to notice and emulate these different traits, habits, and beliefs, I became much more successful myself. It began slowly at first, but the more I practiced and refined my new "system," the more successful I became—and the faster things went.

In fact, I'm sitting in my beautiful beachfront condo on the big island of Hawaii as I write this—something I wouldn't have dared to even dream about before I discovered and refined my "Science of Success."

As I said, I made my initial discovery many years ago, and have spent the last 25 years refining it and teaching it to others. To say that I've become successful using the same system I want to teach you is somewhat of an understatement.

SO PLEASE, FOR YOUR OWN SAKE, PAY ATTENTION!

I've shared the stage and presented with the top success & self-improvement experts in the country—including such notables as: *Zig Ziglar, Robert Schuller, Robert Kiyosaki, Tony Robbins, Brian Tracy, Denis Waitley, Harv Eker, Howard Putnam, Jack Canfield, and John Gray.*

On top of that, some of the top success-minded companies in the country (IBM, Coca Cola, Merrill Lynch, Subway, Sprint, AT&T, Verizon, Century 21, Re/Max, Dow Chemical, Blue Cross/Blue Shield, and many, many more) have hired me to teach their top executives how to become more successful, so you might say I really do "walk the walk," rather than just "talk the talk," like so many others.

By the way, I'm not just talking about financial success, either. I'm talking about true and complete success—success that creates total Harmonic Wealth® and that <u>deep-down peace of mind</u> that comes with it.

Of course, financial success is a big part of it, and any total success system must help you down the road to financial independence. But that's only the beginning.

The real key to creating the life of your dreams is achieving true Harmonic Wealth. That's where you find contentment... peace-of-mind... a deep connection to (and understanding of) the world around you and your place in it.

Let me explain. There are five important kinds of wealth, but none of them (even financial riches) alone can bring you true success or happiness.

Here they are...

FIRST IS FINANCIAL WEALTH.

It's the money in your bank account... the wad of bills in your pocket... your stock portfolio... real-estate holdings... or maybe even just the paycheck you'll pick up next Friday.

THEN THERE'S PHYSICAL WEALTH.

This is the health and fitness of your body. What good is financial wealth if you can't even get around and enjoy it? I've know many wealthy (I mean filthy rich) people who would gladly give up all their financial riches to be able to get their health back or enjoy a reasonable level of fitness.

ANOTHER KIND OF WEALTH IS RELATIONAL WEALTH.

This is the state of your personal relationships (including that with yourself). Again, I've met many who would gladly trade financial wealth for true love or even a good friendship. We are social animals, and we're always healthier and happier when we have rewarding, healthy relationships with others combined with a good level of self-esteem.

AND YET ANOTHER KIND OF WEALTH IS INTELLECTUAL WEALTH.

This is your wealth of knowledge. It's the combination of facts, skills, talents, and life experiences you built up and developed over the years. It's your understanding of how the physical world works.

FINALLY, THERE'S SPIRITUAL WEALTH.

This is that hard-to-define, yet unmistakable-when-you-have-it kind of wealth. It's that (usually) untapped, yet incredibly powerful, almost magical kind of wealth. It's your connection to the rest of the universe and the way you tap into its power. It's the inner energy we all have. It's a major component of contentment and peace-of-mind.

WHEN ALL FIVE OF THESE ARE BALANCED, YOU ACHIEVE HARMONIC WEALTH.

How do I know this?

Remember, I've spent the last 25 years studying every aspect of success, successful people, and building wealth. But I didn't stop at just those who were financially wealthy; I looked for and learned from those who were happy—*and those who weren't!*

I studied and worked with people from all walks of life—professionals, laborers, doctors, lawyers, business people, clergymen, the butcher, the baker and the candlestick maker.

You name it. If it affected success or showed any of the five kinds of wealth, I studied it. I was always looking to see what combinations of the different kinds of wealth and character traits made people happy. *After all, isn't that what we all really want?*

I was amazed to find out that some of them were happy with much less financial resources than I (and maybe you) could get by on, and others made multiple millions a year and still weren't happy.

The simple fact of the matter is that it takes a reasonable level of success and balance between all five kinds of wealth for people to achieve and maintain happiness…

…to become winners… to become truly successful…

…AND TO ACHIEVE TRUE HARMONIC WEALTH.

Once I had mastered the art of success, I became determined to share my discoveries with others. I do this in the form of a weekend training I call the **Harmonic Wealth Weekend**, and I'd like to tell you a little about it and how it could dramatically change your life.

Why am I anxious to share my life's work with you?

Simple…

It's what I love doing… it's a valuable service to my students and clients… it's made me extremely successful (yes, financially wealthy, too)… and it fills my need to help others.

HERE'S A TASTE OF WHAT YOU'LL DISCOVER…

- The areas of your life that are "out of harmony;" what true harmony really means to your results; and how to make immediate corrections…

- The unconscious limitations that have kept you from your unlimited potential…

- How to immediately and exponentially increase your own

energy level...

- The easy way to vanquish stress and fears that have held you stuck in place...

- Your power to create and attract everything you want...

- New internal programming and behavior patterns that will catapult you to your goals...

- How to build habits of thought and action that guarantee your on-going ability to succeed in whatever you set to accomplish...

- A strategic life blueprint for immediate implementation and achievement...

- How to eliminate procrastination—forever...

- If you have an unconscious fear of failure...or even worse (and more common) a fear of success. You'll learn how to blow it away, never to sabotage you again...

- The unvarnished truth about luck (both good and bad) and how it affects your success...

- A nasty little trick your brain plays on you, which can make success nearly impossible to achieve and how to neutralize it once and for all...

- What your TBS is and how a few little changes can have profound effects for the rest of your life...

- And lots, lots more...

AND THAT'S JUST THE TIP OF THE ICEBERG!

Of course, you know *I'm* going to tell you how great the *Harmonic Wealth Weekend* is, because I'm trying to convince you to join me. And, since I make my living by training people like you how to achieve true Harmonic Wealth, you might think I'm a little biased.

So, why not take a look at what a few recent *Harmonic Wealth*

Weekend participants had to say…

"Since working with James and attending the Harmonic Wealth Weekend, my already successful dental practice has increased in business revenue by over 30% and is still climbing with no end in sight! If you want to create true wealth in all areas of your life, you gotta check this guy out."

David I. Peck, DMD

"Since returning from the event, I have attracted a wonderful woman into my life, my health issues have completely cured themselves and my income has increased by 125% in the first 60 days."

Scott Hughes

"Before the Harmonic Wealth Weekend, I was working around the clock and not seeing any results. Since my weekend experience with James, I can finally see the results. I work less, spend more time with my family and have more money in the bank."

Greg Stokes

**FOR MORE INFORMATION ABOUT HOW YOU CAN EXPERIENCE
HARMONIC WEALTH IN ALL AREAS OF YOUR LIFE, VISIT
WWW.HARMONICWEALTHWEEKEND.COM**

THE SCIENCE OF SUCCESS